The Apocalypse

Don Herston

Published by These Glad Tidings Publishing, 2023.

THE APOCALYPSE

First edition. July 7, 2023.

ISBN: 979-8227234308

Written by Don Herston.

Chapter 1– The Real Satan of the Bible

For almost two thousand years, Christians have viewed the Trinity as a three in one God in eternity, and by eternity they usually mean an endless future on the present timeline. This view of the Trinity is believed to be supported by the Bible.

1 John 5:7-8 For there are three that bear record in heaven, the Father, the Word, and the Holy Ghost: and these three are one. And there are three that bear witness in earth, the Spirit, and the water, and the blood: and these three agree in one.

There are other passages of support for the Trinity, but this is the only occasion where the Trinity is presented as a three in one God in Heaven. The Trinity as a three in one God in Heaven is a view that has dominated Christianity largely because of this passage in the First Epistle of John.

But this passage is translated differently in many modern versions of the Bible.

1 John 5:7-8 (English Standard Version) For there are three that testify: the Spirit and the water and the blood; and these three agree.

The part about a three in one God in Heaven has been eliminated because it is not found in the earlier manuscripts.

Could God have allowed the Bible to be altered? This is one of the very few occasions where there appears to have been a change in the Biblical text. In this case the alteration helped to conceal the true explanation for the Trinity, and the error was exposed centuries ago, so that the true word of God has been preserved. The inerrancy of the Bible does not require that every translation of the Bible be inerrant.

Many Christians still believe in the erroneous text that was not found in the earlier manuscripts. All Christians seem to believe in the idea of a three in one God in Heaven that was supported by this error.

There is no Biblical support for the idea that the Trinity is a three in one God in Heaven. There is an explanation for the Trinity that involves a completely different structure.

Today, with the confirmation of the Big Bang, we can understand God as the uncaused cause outside of time and space. This view seems more likely since it means that God transcends time and not the other way around, but it is improbable that such a timeless God would be divided into parts. A timeless God would almost certainly have the simplest structure possible which would be one supernatural Almighty I AM. This would be God the Father.

The God of the Bible is outside of time, but in some Biblical stories God seems to move in time. This is completely reasonable if both are true. God the Father can be outside of time, while God the Son exists in time. This is a better explanation for the Trinity since the uncaused cause would be outside of time, but we know Jesus exists in time. He came into the world and lived as a human.

Mark 13:32 But of that day and that hour knoweth no man, no, not the angels which are in heaven, neither the Son, but the Father.

Jesus said that only the Father knows the time of the end, but it makes no sense that God the Father would be keeping a secret from God the Son. Christians focus entirely on the end-time aspect of this statement which distracts them from what Jesus is saying. Only God the Father transcends time. God the Father knows, or is one with, all moments on the timeline while Jesus is God moving through time. This view of the relationship between the Father and the Son explains how Jesus can be God while there is only one God.

I believe in one God, the Father almighty, maker of heaven and earth, of all things visible and invisible.

There is one God, the Father, outside of time.

I believe in one Lord Jesus Christ, the Only Begotten Son of God, born of the Father before all ages. God from God, Light from Light, true God from true God, begotten, not made, consubstantial with the Father; through him all things were made.

Jesus was "begotten" of the Father, from the same substance, before all ages so there was never "a time" when Jesus did not exist. All of this is best explained by Christ being a consciousness of God that came into time and space the moment God the Father created time and space. Constructing the universe and the other levels of reality would be executed over time, so it would be the Son of God managing the creation of all things. The Son of God moves in time, but He has power over time by which He would almost certainly have knowledge of the day and hour of His return.

The mind or consciousness of God is far beyond our ability to comprehend, but there would have to be a significant degree of separation between God the Father, outside of time, and God the Son, inside time and space. Yet still, it is one God who exists outside of time, and He moves though the time He created.

God the Father outside of time and God the Son moving in time would be a good explanation for the Trinity, but there is a third member of the Trinity. Only God the Father is outside of time, so there must be a way and a reason for God to have more than one consciousness moving through time.

I believe in the Holy Spirit, the Lord, the giver of life, who proceeds from the Father and the Son.

The Son of God is begotten, but the Holy Spirit proceeds from God. Both words suggest coming from God. The Holy Spirit would have to exist in time like the Son of God but would be a different consciousness if the Holy Spirit exists at a different level of reality. Since the Holy Spirit proceeds from both the Father and the Son, the Son exists at a higher level of reality than the Holy Spirit.

The Holy Spirit is in Heaven, while the Son of God is at a level of reality that transcends Heaven referred to as the Right Hand of God. This transcending level of Heaven has been kept secret even from the inhabitants of Heaven. The Son of God came down to a lower level of reality when He was born as a human, but He continued to exist at the Right Hand of God, and He returned fully to the Right Hand of God after His resurrection.

The Right Hand of God is a transcending level of Heaven. This is not to say that every time the Bible mentions the right hand of God it is talking about this transcending dimension. This does not deny that Jesus came from Heaven and returned to Heaven. Jesus is in a place that transcends the angels and all the inhabitants of Heaven. It has been kept secret. It is the highest level of Heaven. It transcends the rest of Heaven just as Heaven transcends the Earth.

As far as Heaven with angels and the throne of God, John described a vision of Heaven in the book of Revelation and there is no mention of a Lamb.

Revelation 4:4-5 And round about the throne were four and twenty seats: and upon the seats I saw four and twenty elders sitting, clothed in white raiment; and they had on their heads crowns of gold. And out of the throne proceeded lightnings and thunderings and voices: and there were seven lamps of fire burning before the throne, which are the seven Spirits of God.

In the fifth chapter we learn of a book sealed with seven seals that no man could open.

Revelation 5:3 And no man in heaven, nor in earth, neither under the earth, was able to open the book, neither to look thereon.

Jesus ascended in His body, so He is still fully God and fully human. Jesus was not in this level of Heaven described by John because no man in Heaven could open the book. In the previous chapter when John described the throne and the elders, there was no mention of a Lamb.

After being told there was someone who could open the book, John looks again at the throne. Only this time, there is a Lamb.

Revelation 5:6 And I beheld, and, lo, in the midst of the throne and of the four beasts, and in the midst of the elders, stood a Lamb as it had been slain, having seven horns and seven eyes, which are the seven Spirits of God sent forth into all the earth.

John looked at the throne and the elders, the same scene he described in the fourth chapter. In the fifth chapter a Lamb seems to suddenly appear. Previously no man in Heaven could open the book, because previously there was no Lamb. Christ came from a transcending level of Heaven. He came into this level of Heaven where there is the throne and the elders.

It is a bit confusing since the passage calls Christ a Lion, and later He is called a Lamb. This is a remarkably effective distraction as the text is clearly referring to Jesus who is fully God and fully human. As will be shown later, it is this monumental event when Christ comes into this level of Heaven that the devil is cast out of Heaven.

It is the revelation of the Son of God in Heaven that causes the devil to be cast out of Heaven.

Since He is the Lord, it should not be revolutionary to say that Jesus transcends Heaven. If Jesus has not yet revealed Himself in Heaven, the inhabitants of Heaven would only know Jesus as a human who died a long time ago.

The devil is still in Heaven because the devil is not at war with God, the devil is at war with us. For the devil to be at war with God would be like a character in a novel doing battle with the author. God has all power, and the only power Satan has is what God allows him to have. Perhaps the devil is stupid enough to be openly hostile to God, but it seems unlikely that the devil would be that stupid.

It is odd that so many people for so many centuries would believe without question that the devil is at war with God. God has all power, and the devil has no power. Somehow there is such a struggle that the devil is cast out of Heaven, and he still battles with God for possession of souls. This is not to question the Bible since this view is not supported by the Bible.

Other than some clues that he will be cast out of Heaven, the Old Testament does not present the devil as openly evil. The devil may have misled Eve to destroy her, but nothing he said was false.

God transcends time. God knew that all humans would sin, that they would be overcome by the devil and would experience death. What God told Adam and Eve was completely true.

> *Genesis 3:4-5 And the serpent said unto the woman, Ye shall not surely die: For God doth know that in the day ye eat thereof, then your eyes shall be opened, and ye shall be as gods, knowing good and evil.*

Satan does not transcend time, so he is not a witness to the future. The devil did not bear false witness. The devil pointed out that it is entirely up to us to overcome his influence. Whether or not we sin is entirely up to us. Whether or not we die is entirely up to us.

The devil said that Adam and Eve would be like the "gods"; they would be like the spirits of Heaven as Adam and Eve would be able to "know" (be one with) good and evil spirits. The spirits of Heaven can know or share consciousness with each other in a way that physical humans cannot. After the disobedience of the humans, the good and evil spirits would be allowed to be one with or to influence the humans. Satan wanted to influence and thereby destroy the humans, so his statement was malicious and deceptive, but it was not actually false.

Satan is powerful and very intelligent. The devil tested Job with permission from God. The Satan of the Bible is never openly sinful or openly hostile to God.

There is no occasion in the Old Testament where the devil openly committed a sin. This is because the devil knows he is powerless next to God, and any hostility on his part would have to be kept under control. All the evil spirits must conceal their hatred of God. The absence of sin on the part of Satan shows that the devil is not in open conflict with God. Common sense tells us that Satan is not likely stupid enough to be in open conflict with God. This suggests that the devil has not yet been cast out of Heaven.

Genesis 6:1-2 And it came to pass, when men began to multiply on the face of the earth, and daughters were born unto them, That the sons of God saw the daughters of men that they were fair; and they took them wives of all which they chose.

In Genesis the "sons" of God came to the Earth, and this happened a long time ago, but this passage does not mention Satan. There is no reason to believe that Satan was cast out of Heaven at that time. Satan continued to refrain from sin or any open hostility towards God after this event.

In the New Testament it becomes clear that the devil is evil, but there is still nothing to suggest that Satan is openly evil or openly hostile to God. There is still, even in the New Testament, no occasion where the devil openly committed a sin. Satan is certainly hostile to humanity, but the devil seems to have the intelligence and the willpower to keep his hatred of God to himself.

Since the devil is ultimately cast out of Heaven, his hatred of God was or will be exposed at some point.

There are other passages in the Old Testament that seem to describe Satan being cast out of Heaven. They are almost never clear as to when Satan is cast out. As will be shown later, there is one passage in the book of Isaiah that does provide a clue as to the timing.

The following passage in Ezekiel seems to be talking about the devil being cast out of Heaven, but it is not clear concerning the timing.

Ezekiel 28:14-16 Thou art the anointed cherub that covereth; and I have set thee so: thou wast upon the holy mountain of God; thou hast walked up and down in the midst of the stones of fire. Thou wast perfect in thy ways from the day that thou wast created, till iniquity was found in thee. By the multitude of thy merchandise they have filled the midst of thee with violence, and thou hast sinned: therefore I will cast thee as profane out of the mountain of God: and I will destroy thee, O covering cherub, from the midst of the stones of fire.

This passage says that the devil "was upon the holy mountain" which is past tense. It later says, "I will cast thee as profane out of the holy mountain" which is future tense. This passage sounds like a declaration that was or will be made by God at that most climactic moment when God casts Satan out of Heaven. There is no clear indication as to when that occurred or will occur.

Once God declares that He is going to cast Satan out of Heaven, the casting out would occur almost immediately. Satan would be openly hostile after being told that he is going to be cast out. There would be no reason to keep an openly hostile spirit in Heaven. Since the devil is not openly hostile, it seems as though he has not yet been cast out of Heaven.

The devil is not openly hostile because he believes he has everything under control. Satan is extremely arrogant. God never clearly revealed through the prophets how He will destroy the devil. This passage in Ezekiel about an "anointed cherub" being cast from the "mountain of God" is vague. There are many clues that must be pieced together. The devil is not concerned with this enigmatic statement made by the puny little human named Ezekiel. Satan has absolutely no respect for humans, and no idea what God is planning.

It is clear in this passage that Satan has not openly rebelled against God. The passage says that he was perfect in his ways until iniquity was found in him. This means Satan did not openly sin. Satan was hiding iniquity, perhaps he was full of hatred, but not openly expressing any hostility. This passage confirms that there was iniquity hidden within Satan. At some point, the evil that Satan is hiding was or will be exposed.

Proverbs 26:24-26 He that hateth dissembleth with his lips, and layeth up deceit within him; When he speaketh fair, believe him not: for there are seven abominations in his heart. Whose hatred is covered by deceit, his wickedness shall be shewed before the whole congregation.

Surely Satan exercises restraint since God has all power, but his iniquity will be exposed. The Biblical Satan does not battle God for possession of souls. The Biblical Satan condemns humanity. As the devil condemns humanity, he must do so without being caught violating the Law of God. Satan may be much bigger than the Earth, but he is subject to the Law of God. This is undeniable since the devil is ultimately condemned by the Law of God.

Revelation 20:10 And the devil that deceived them was cast into the lake of fire and brimstone, where the beast and the false prophet are, and shall be tormented day and night for ever and ever.

Psalms 82:1 God standeth in the congregation of the mighty; he judgeth among the gods.

According to the Bible, Satan presents himself as an angel of righteousness.

2 Corinthians 11:14 And no marvel; for Satan himself is transformed into an angel of light.

The devil is like a prosecuting attorney demanding justice. Satan keeps his own hatred of God hidden within himself while he stands before God condemning humans for their sins.

There are only two passages in the Bible that indicate the timing of the devil being cast from Heaven. One passage, as will be shown later, is in the book of Isaiah. The other passage is in the book of Revelation. The devil is cast out near the time of the end when there is only a short time left.

Revelation 12:12 Therefore rejoice, ye heavens, and ye that dwell in them. Woe to the inhabiters of the earth and of the sea! for the devil is come down unto you, having great wrath, because he knoweth that he hath but a short time.

If one verse in the Bible says that X is true, and there are other verses indicating that X might be true or Y might be true, this would mean that X is true. People will believe that Y is true if that is what they have always been told. But if one verse says that X is true, and that verse is not actually contradicted by another verse then X must be true.

We would have to say that the devil appears to be cast out of Heaven near the time of the end. Two passages indicate that to be the case. No other passage gives a clear indication as to any other timing for Satan to be cast from Heaven.

Jesus did say that the devil was a liar and a murderer from the beginning.

John 8:44 Ye are of your father the devil, and the lusts of your father ye will do. He was a murderer from the beginning, and abode not in the truth, because there is no truth in him. When he speaketh a lie, he speaketh of his own: for he is a liar, and the father of it.

Satan was a murderer, in that he was full of hatred, and he was also a liar who concealed his hatred, but the devil kept his iniquity hidden. His hatred and his lies had not yet been exposed. Satan may have been evil from the beginning, but he was not exposed as evil from the beginning, this is confirmed in many passages. Jesus did not say that the devil was exposed as a murderer from the beginning, but only that the devil was a murderer from the beginning. Jesus came into the world to expose Satan, but God the Father transcends time, so God already knew the outcome.

Luke 10:18 And he said unto them, I beheld Satan as lightning fall from heaven.

Jesus did not say that Satan has already been cast from Heaven. Jesus stated that He saw Satan fall from Heaven. This could have been a vision of a future event. This verse is not actually clear concerning the timing.

John 12:31 Now is the judgment of this world: now shall the prince of this world be cast out.

We know Christ was describing a vision of a future event since He would later say that the prince of this world shall be cast out. Notice that the casting out "shall be" (in the future) because of something which occurs "now" (at the time of Christ). Satan keeps his hatred hidden within himself. At the time of Christ that evil was exposed so that Satan "shall be" cast out of Heaven sometime in the future.

Hebrews 2:14 Forasmuch then as the children are partakers of flesh and blood, he also himself likewise took part of the same; that through death he might destroy him that had the power of death, that is, the devil;

It is Christ who destroys the devil, and the devil is destroyed by the exposure of his hidden iniquity. Christ must be the one who witnessed the hatred of the devil. That occurred at the crucifixion since Christ destroys Satan through death.

In the book of Luke, it was foretold that Christ would reveal the thoughts of many hearts. If Christ revealed the thoughts of many hearts, then someone was hiding their thoughts. Satan and his angels hide their hatred of God.

Luke 2:34-35 And Simeon blessed them, and said unto Mary his mother, Behold, this child is set for the fall and rising again of many in Israel; and for a sign which shall be spoken against; (Yea, a sword shall pierce through thy own soul also,) that the thoughts of many hearts may be revealed.

Simeon was speaking to both Mary and Jesus. The heart of Mary was pierced, but it was the piercing of the soul of Jesus that revealed the thoughts of many hearts. The sword that pierced the soul of Christ was a spiritual or verbal attack on Christ. This attack revealed hatred that had been hidden. That hatred is what the devil poured out on Christ.

Matthew 27:46 And about the ninth hour Jesus cried with a loud voice, saying, Eli, Eli, lama sabachthani? that is to say, My God, my God, why hast thou forsaken me?

When Christ was on the cross, He clearly stated that God had forsaken Him. He was quoting Scripture but by quoting Scripture, Jesus was quoting Himself. That He was repeating His own words should put more emphasis on this statement. This was the Messiah hanging on a cross between Heaven and Earth, the pivotal event of all creation.

The Lord and Savior was not merely expressing His feelings. With this question Jesus was making an incredibly profound statement concerning an event that had been foretold in the Scriptures. Jesus knew the answer to the question. He asked the question to emphasize that there was an answer. There was a reason for God to forsake Him.

Many demons have openly cursed God and been cast out of Heaven. The more powerful demons have managed to contain their hatred of God, so they remain in Heaven. There may have been times when God looked away as from a great evil, resulting in an area of time and space that is not in the view of God. The powerful demonic spirits would be attracted to these places where they can release some of their pent-up hatred of God.

Jesus was naked and bloodied. He was displayed on the cross like a mounted dead butterfly. There can be no better example of a puny little human the egocentric demons had no reason to fear.

When Christ was dying on the cross, God looked away, and the devil did not know that Jesus was more than a mere human. When God looked away, the powerful demonic spirits rushed to the crucifixion to curse God. God had looked away, but Jesus transcends Heaven.

Imagine looking at a world of only two dimensions. It would be a flat world with flat two-dimensional creatures. The flat creatures in this flat world would not be able to comprehend a third dimension. You could greatly affect their two dimensioned world without leaving your three dimensioned world. You could do great harm to them. As you stand looking at their flat world, they could not detect you, nor even comprehend your existence. This is because you transcend their two dimensioned world.

Likewise, Satan is a spirit who transcended and was looking down on this puny little human dying on a cross. At the same time, Christ also existed at a level of reality that transcends our world and the spirit world. The Son of God transcended and was watching the devil look down on the crucifixion. The devil did not know that Jesus was able to witness his hatred of God. To this day the devil still does not know that Jesus is the Lord because Jesus transcends Heaven.

Genesis 3:15 And I will put enmity between thee and the woman, and between thy seed and her seed; it shall bruise thy head, and thou shalt bruise his heel.

It must be true that the devil does some type of harm to Jesus. This harm would not be the crucifixion itself since that was done by the Romans. Satan bruises His heel, so the devil strikes Jesus in some way. A person's only weakness is called their Achilles' heel. There is no weakness or difficulty for the Lord other than His revulsion to evil.

We cannot begin to understand the immeasurable suffering of Christ. He was subjected to a supernatural level of hatred coming from all demonic spirits. It is believed Christ descended into hell, and this could be because Jesus descended into hell on the cross.

We also cannot know how long the spiritual attack against the Lord lasted. Some demons would be more cautious than others. One by one, they all exposed their hatred of God until they were all condemned.

Deuteronomy 21:23 His body shall not remain all night upon the tree, but thou shalt in any wise bury him that day; (for he that is hanged is accursed of God;) that thy land be not defiled, which the Lord thy God giveth thee for an inheritance.

Galatians 3:13 Christ hath redeemed us from the curse of the law, being made a curse for us: for it is written, Cursed is every one that hangeth on a tree:

The curse on anyone who hangs from a tree is pointing to the crucifixion, and it is pointing to the supernatural suffering of Christ. Being cursed does suggest a descent to hell.

There are the sorrowful mysteries of Christ, those being the agony in the garden, the scourging, crowning with thorns, carrying of the cross and the crucifixion. By far the greatest sorrowful mystery has been kept secret. The real sorrowful agony of Christ went far beyond any physical pain. It was a suffering so great as to make the rest of the Passion unnoticeable. When He was dying on the cross, Jesus experienced the curse of all the hatred of hell.

Since Jesus is fully human, His emotions are exposed in His flesh like when sorrow caused Him to weep. Jesus is the Lord with infinite willpower, but He was so distressed by the cross that He was sweating blood beforehand. Before the crucifixion, the Almighty God was sweeting blood. In His infinite willpower, He could endure anything, but He was also fully human. It was His human soul and body that responded to the pending torment in this way.

The pending torment was not the physical pain. The physical pain of the crucifixion would be nothing to the Lord. It would be something that the Lord could easily overcome. On the cross, Jesus was responding to the evil He was a witness to, but the crucifixion did conceal His ability to witness the hatred of the devil. He looked like a human responding to the pain of the cross.

We are redeemed by the crucifixion, and the crucifixion is another reason God created the world. On the cross, God put Himself in a position where He was forced to confront evil. God was forced to make an unbelievably incredible sacrifice to express His love and to save His children from death.

Christ witnessed the evil of Satan, and this is why He is called the faithful witness.

Revelation 1:5 And from Jesus Christ, who is the faithful witness, and the first begotten of the dead, and the prince of the kings of the earth. Unto him that loved us, and washed us from our sins in his own blood,

When Christ was dying on the cross, the devil exposed his hatred of God. As will be shown, this causes a lot of clues to fit together. This is the attack on Christ that revealed the thoughts of Satan and all the other demonic spirits. The devil hid his hatred, but "now" (at the time of Christ) the evil within Satan is exposed. The devil "shall be" cast out at some point in the future.

Satan has not yet been cast out of Heaven because it has been kept secret that the devil was caught in a violation of the Law of God. Satan unloaded his hatred on Christ and yet God has miraculously prevented billions of Christians from seeing it.

In this next verse there is a verbal attack on someone who is perfect. This attack comes from "workers of iniquity" who believe that no one is watching.

Psalm 64:3-5 Who whet their tongue like a sword, and bend their bows to shoot their arrows, even bitter words: That they may shoot in secret at the perfect: suddenly do they shoot at him, and fear not. They encourage themselves in an evil matter: they commune of laying snares privily; they say, Who shall see them?

An attack on someone who is perfect while no one is watching would be an attack on Christ when God turned His face from the crucifixion. The devil unloaded his hatred of God on a dying Christ. This is how the devil bruised the heel of Jesus, but this is also how Jesus defeated the devil.

Satan and his angels feared not. This is because God had looked away and the devil did not realize that Christ is God who transcends Heaven.

Psalms 22:16-18 For dogs have compassed me: the assembly of the wicked have inclosed me: they pierced my hands and my feet. I may tell all my bones: they look and stare upon me. They part my garments among them, and cast lots upon my vesture.

This Psalm describes the crucifixion in remarkable detail. The dogs were the Roman soldiers, but in this same passage Jesus was also surrounded by much larger "bulls". The bulls attacked Christ verbally (or spiritually). This would be Satan and his angels.

Psalms 22:12-13 Many bulls have compassed me: strong bulls of Bashan have beset me round. They gaped upon me with their mouths, as a ravening and a roaring lion.

Notice what Christ said about those who hate Him.

John 15:22-25 If I had not come and spoken unto them, they had not had sin: but now they have no cloak for their sin. He that hateth me hateth my Father also. If I had not done among them the works which none other man did, they had not had sin: but now have they both seen and hated both me and my Father. But this cometh to pass, that the word might be fulfilled that is written in their law, They hated me without a cause.

This passage was used in the past to justify the persecution of Jews. Today, Christians often avoid this passage because of the violence committed in the past by those who clearly misinterpreted what Christ was saying. It should be obvious that this passage is not talking about the Jews. Did Jews not have sin before Christ came into the world?

Yet Christians cannot disregard this passage. These are the words of Christ. There is someone who did not have sin before Christ came into the world, but they now have sin because of His coming into the world. The sin that they now have is hatred of God. "Their law" in this passage is reference to Satan and his angels using the Law of God to condemn humans. They used the sins of humanity to justify their hostility towards humanity, but they have no excuse for their hatred of God. They are condemned by the same Law they used to condemn humanity.

Psalms 109:3 They compassed me about also with words of hatred; and fought against me without a cause.

Satan can condemn humans for their sins, but the hatred directed at Christ by Satan was hatred without a cause. The devil exposed his hatred of God.

Psalms 110:1 The Lord said unto my Lord, Sit thou at my right hand, until I make thine enemies thy footstool.

Christ will be at the "right hand" of God until His enemies are made His footstool. The relationship of Christ at the Right Hand of God will come to an end and the enemies of God will be made His footstool. These are two different events, but they occur at the same time because one causes the other. Christ will no longer sit at the Right Hand of God because He will go into Heaven. Perhaps He will return to the Earth revealing Himself to be the Son of God. His appearance in Heaven, or maybe a revelation prior to His appearance, will cause His enemies to be His footstool.

Isaiah 66:1 Thus saith the Lord, The heaven is my throne, and the earth is my footstool: where is the house that ye build unto me? and where is the place of my rest?

The Earth is His footstool, and the devil is cast out into the Earth.

The following passage is believed to be about the antichrist as it is talking about a man.

2 Thessalonians 2:3-8 Let no man deceive you by any means: for that day shall not come, except there come a falling away first, and that man of sin be revealed, the son of perdition; Who opposeth and exalteth himself above all that is called God, or that is worshipped; so that he as God sitteth in the temple of God, shewing himself that he is God. Remember ye not, that, when I was yet with you, I told you these things? And now ye know what withholdeth that he might be revealed in his time. For the mystery of iniquity doth already work: only he who now letteth will let, until he be taken out of the way. And then shall that Wicked be revealed, whom the Lord shall consume with the spirit of his mouth, and shall destroy with the brightness of his coming:

He is not literally the son of perdition; destruction is not literally his mother. The son of perdition is merely a title. Man of sin is also a title. A dedicated nurse may be called an angel of mercy, but she is not literally an angel. A demon like Satan may be called a "man of sin" even if he is not a man. This passage is another clue that what comes before the end is the revealing of the sin of Satan.

Satan is the Wicked that is revealed or exposed and consumed by the spirit of the Lord's mouth, consumed by the testimony of Christ.

In the book of Job there is a lot of discussion about suffering, and why God allows the righteous Job to suffer. When God answered Job, God spoke of the leviathan. The leviathan is a sea monster, or a dragon and it represents Satan. In answering the question of evil and suffering, God is declaring that He will destroy evil. By asking Job if he can do these things to Satan, God is showing what He will do to Satan.

Job 41:1-2 Canst thou draw out leviathan with an hook? or his tongue with a cord which thou lettest down? Canst thou put an hook into his nose? or bore his jaw through with a thorn?

God catches Satan with a "hook" meaning Satan does not openly rebel, but he is caught in a trap. This trap would be Christ on the cross who is the witness against Satan. It is the tongue of Satan that is caught, and this is because the demonic verbal attack against Christ by the devil is how Christ destroys the devil. The Messiah was "lettest down", which is to say sent down to the Earth to trap the devil.

Job 41:3-4 Will he make many supplications unto thee? will he speak soft words unto thee? Will he make a covenant with thee? wilt thou take him for a servant for ever?

These two verses are remarkable. Here we see the cunning Satan before the throne of God, not in open rebellion, but speaking softly and seeking a covenant with God. Satan secretly hates God, and he knows that his hatred of God will lead to his downfall. Satan wants God to agree to keep him as a servant forever.

Job 41:5-6 Wilt thou play with him as with a bird? or wilt thou bind him for thy maidens? Shall the companions make a banquet of him? shall they part him among the merchants?

Here God binds Satan. The book of Revelation says that Satan will be bound for a thousand years.

Job 41:12-17 I will not conceal his parts, nor his power, nor his comely proportion. Who can discover the face of his garment? or who can come to him with his double bridle? Who can open the doors of his face? his teeth are terrible round about. His scales are his pride, shut up together as with a close seal. One is so near to another, that no air can come between them. They are joined one to another, they stick together, that they cannot be sundered.

Here we see how Satan keeps his hatred hidden within himself. We see in this passage the great willpower of Satan. Satan keeps his heart powerfully sealed. Who is the one who discovers the face of Satan's garment, who opens the doors of his face? That would be Christ, who exposes the evil of Satan.

Isaiah 27:1 In that day the Lord with his sore and great and strong sword shall punish leviathan the piercing serpent, even leviathan that crooked serpent; and he shall slay the dragon that is in the sea.

Isaiah also speaks of the leviathan and indicates a judgment for the devil that will take place in the future. Not only in the future, the wording in this chapter of Isaiah, and the previous chapter, suggests that this takes place at the time of the end. There is a great trumpet being blown, and a woman with child about to deliver her baby.

Isaiah 26:18 We have been with child, we have been in pain, we have as it were brought forth wind; we have not wrought any deliverance in the earth; neither have the inhabitants of the world fallen.

Isaiah 26:21 For, behold, the Lord cometh out of his place to punish the inhabitants of the earth for their iniquity: the earth also shall disclose her blood, and shall no more cover her slain.

Isaiah 27:13 And it shall come to pass in that day, that the great trumpet shall be blown, and they shall come which were ready to perish in the land of Assyria, and the outcasts in the land of Egypt, and shall worship the Lord in the holy mount at Jerusalem.

Very subtle and enigmatic, but this passage is the only clue in the Old Testament concerning the timing of Satan being cast out of Heaven. It agrees with the only New Testament clue found in the book of Revelation. Satan is cast out of Heaven at the time of the end.

Revelation 12:12 Therefore rejoice, ye heavens, and ye that dwell in them. Woe to the inhabiters of the earth and of the sea! for the devil is come down unto you, having great wrath, because he knoweth that he hath but a short time.

When Satan is cast out of Heaven, he knows that he has but a short time meaning he now knows that he is doomed. Satan could not have known of his doom before that time. If Satan had previously known he was doomed, he would have previously had great wrath. There would have previously been conflict in Heaven. Once Satan knows that he is doomed there will be conflict in Heaven.

As a witness, Christ testifies against the devil, and that testimony is figuratively a sword coming out of His mouth.

Revelation 1:16 And he had in his right hand seven stars: and out of his mouth went a sharp twoedged sword: and his countenance was as the sun shineth in his strength.

In this next verse the Messiah's mouth is like a sword, and it also describes the Messiah as being hidden. Jesus is at the Right Hand of God, a transcending level of Heaven. He has been kept hidden from the inhabitants of Heaven. The Messiah is compared to a shaft hidden in a quiver that will be fired when the time comes.

Isaiah 49:2 And he hath made my mouth like a sharp sword; in the shadow of his hand hath he hid me, and made me a polished shaft; in his quiver hath he hid me;

The secret place is the "Right Hand of God", a place that transcends Heaven where the Son of God has been kept secret from the inhabitants of Heaven.

Psalm 91:1 He that dwelleth in the secret place of the most High shall abide under the shadow of the Almighty.

The judgment of the Lord is far above and out of the sight of the devil, or unknown to the devil.

Psalm 10:4-6 The wicked, through the pride of his countenance, will not seek after God: God is not in all his thoughts. His ways are always grievous; thy judgments are far above out of his sight: as for all his enemies, he puffeth at them. He hath said in his heart, I shall not be moved: for I shall never be in adversity.

It will be revealed in Heaven that Jesus is Lord, and this will lead to a war, or more of a debate, between the archangel Michael and the devil. The devil will be cast from Heaven.

Revelation 12:7-8 And there was war in heaven: Michael and his angels fought against the dragon; and the dragon fought and his angels, And prevailed not; neither was their place found any more in heaven.

The revelation of the Messiah is when it is revealed in Heaven that Jesus is Lord. We cannot know when or how these events will unfold in Heaven, and the devil is extremely arrogant. Satan will not quickly entertain the notion that he has been brought down by a human. It would be like being told that a bug you once stepped on many years ago is still alive and is going to testify against you.

Luke 17:29-30 But the same day that Lot went out of Sodom it rained fire and brimstone from heaven, and destroyed them all. Even thus shall it be in the day when the Son of man is revealed.

When it is revealed in Heaven that Jesus is the Lord, and He is at a transcending level of Heaven, then the devil will know he is doomed. A great disaster, like what happened to Sodom, will happen when the Son of man is revealed. The revelation of the Messiah in Heaven will cause the devil to be cast out of Heaven into the Earth.

This is the surprise party that God has in store for Satan. Satan does not know, nor has he considered, that the human Jesus is the Lord, still alive in a place that transcends Heaven. The devil saw Christ as an imperfect human like all the rest. The Christians came to believe that Christ is part of a three in one God in Heaven, an idea which Satan knows to be false. Once the devil realizes that Christ is the Lord, then the devil will know that he is doomed.

In his great arrogance, the devil will not take this seriously.

But when Satan does take this seriously, there will be a battle, a debate between him and the Archangel Michael. Shown to be guilty, the devil will be cast out of Heaven.

Numbers 10:35 And it came to pass, when the ark set forward, that Moses said, Rise up, Lord, and let thine enemies be scattered; and let them that hate thee flee before thee.

Jesus is at the Right Hand of God, and Jesus is the Right Hand of God.

Psalms 21:8 Thine hand shall find out all thine enemies: thy right hand shall find out those that hate thee.

Chapter 2 – A Summary

We put little thought into very fundamental questions like what is the purpose of Creation? Christians do not normally describe creation as a trial or a test, but they believe that God gave us the freedom to love Him or not love Him. Christians believe God gave us free will, which is the ability to be good or evil, and God judges us at the end of the world based on our choices. This means Christians believe that creation is a test even if they never consider the question of why God created the world. This book argues that the world is not a test. To realize and fully embrace the idea that creation is not a test results in a completely different view of God and the Bible.

To achieve the real purpose of creation, God had to create humans who struggle between good and evil. We must be evil to sin and be worthy of death. We must be compassionate to feel sorrow for those who die, so that God can experience sorrow through us.

A loving God would want to experience sorrow. Sorrow requires suffering. A perfectly righteous God would create the conditions where He is not the cause of suffering. God allows us to cause suffering because it is essential for God to know what love is, but then God responds to the suffering that we cause. Some people cause more suffering, and God will punish them. Some people suffer more than they deserve, and God will repay them.

There is a Day of Judgment, but the world was not created for the purpose of judgment. God created a world where evil would form, resulting in a struggle between good and evil. The Day of Judgment is when God destroys evil.

Punishment for sin comes before the Day of Judgment and is sometimes called temporal judgment. Punishment for sin before the

Day of Judgment, and the destruction of evil on the Day of Judgment are two different objectives. They are both essential to a righteous God as a response to suffering. Understanding these two objectives explains conflicting Bible passages.

God created a world of good and evil for God to be able to experience emotions. God created angels, demons, and humans outside of Himself, giving them the ability to act as "free agents". Angels, demons, and humans act freely, independent of God, causing suffering.

God created loving angels, but God also created loveless demons, including some who were given great power like Satan. The demons became evil as foreknown. God then created a tiny little rock called the Earth, floating in a vast universe. The Earth is remarkably insignificant relative to Heaven. Humans were made as weak spirits attached to flesh, but most humans were given a righteous spirit of love. Humans are like angels and demons, only smaller, weaker, and attached to fleshly bodies.

There is no battle between the good and evil spirits in Heaven. The angels are repulsed by the demons, and the demons hate God and the angels. This means both sides are repulsed by the other side, but the demons must conceal their hatred. There is a separation between the good and evil spirits like the yin and yang of Chinese philosophy, but God transcends all existence and God exercises complete control. The demons must conceal their hatred or be removed from Heaven, but they can have a great impact on the Earth.

The only conflict between the good and evil spirits is disagreement, and how they influence creatures on the Earth.

Satan is still in Heaven since he has great power, and he stays within the Law of God even as he came to secretly hate God. We are both good and evil because we are loving spirits attached to flesh. Our flesh is influenced by powerful evil spirits causing us to violate the Law. Satan hates God but the devil can do no harm to God. God loves the humans, so Satan destroys the humans. This is exactly what God had in mind. This is how God has creatures who struggle between good and evil.

God allowed Satan to corrupt the material world. We owe our existence to Satan, and we struggle between good and evil because of the influence of the devil. Satan is part of us most of the time. When we are selfish or angry God is repulsed and will watch us from a distance.

When we are righteous, contrite, or sorrowful, God is within our mind and soul. In our most difficult times, God feels precisely what we feel. God has felt the sorrow, loneliness, and anxiety of all His children throughout time. This is how creation provides God with a full understanding of what love is. This is why God created the world.

God created spirits and humans, outside of Himself, with free agency. God allows humans influenced by the devil to cause suffering, and humans are the cause of most suffering. Satan is the source of evil, but humans are the manifestation of evil.

The devil is a bad influence on humanity, but Satan does not violate the Law of God, nor directly cause any suffering. God foreknew there would be suffering, but God also foreknew that in the end He will redeem all love and destroy all evil.

The early church believed that Christ redeems us by defeating death, or by defeating the devil, or by freeing us from the dominion of Satan. This is called Christus Victor. Christus Victor is the name of a book by Gustaf Aulen, first published in 1931, which showed that this is what the early church believed. The ransom theory emerged as the explanation for how Christ frees us from the dominion of Satan.

Over a thousand years after Christ, the church in western Europe moved away from the ransom theory. The Church not only abandon the ransom theory, but they also abandon the idea that Christ redeems us by freeing us from the dominion of Satan. Instead, they embraced the idea that Christ redeems us by His righteousness and/or His suffering being somehow applied to us.

This led to satisfaction atonement for Catholicism which would eventually lead to substitution atonement or penal substitution for protestants. The problem with both satisfaction atonement and substitutionary atonement is that they are both clearly and repeatedly rejected by the Jewish Scriptures. God does not punish anyone for the sins of someone else.

We may be "healed by His stripes", but it cannot be true that our sins, or our dishonoring of God is satisfied by the righteousness, or the suffering of the Messiah being applied to us. Everyone will be judged for their own words and actions; the Bible is clear on this. Substitution atonement espouses a means of redemption that contradicts the Bible and rejects what the early church believed.

We are healed by His stripes because the suffering of Christ somehow defeats death or frees us from the dominion of Satan. Ransom theory tried to explain how Christ defeated the devil. Just because ransom theory is a bad explanation, that does not mean there cannot be some other explanation. The redemption provided to us by Christ must be consistent with the Jewish Scriptures.

There are two parts to our redemption. The two parts to our redemption are represented by the bread and wine of the Last Supper. They are also represented by the blood and water that flowed from the side of Christ. To understand the two parts of our redemption we must first understand the Trinity.

The Trinity is best explained by pointing out that God is both outside of time and moving in time, but Trinity means three. There must be a second consciousness of God moving in time. There is God the Father outside of time, and there are two manifestations of God within time and space. These two manifestations of God exist in two different realms or two different levels of reality. The two levels of reality would be parallel to each other, or one would transcend the other. God could not allow this explanation for the Trinity to be explored until near the time of the end. This conversation would lead to the idea that Jesus transcends Heaven. This is something that had to be kept secret.

While the Holy Spirit is in Heaven, the Son of God is at a transcending level of Heaven called the Right Hand of God.

Satan has great willpower and is still in Heaven, but Jesus transcends that level of Heaven. Even when He walked the Earth, Jesus existed at a transcending level of Heaven. Jesus had a body and a soul that were fully human, but He also continued to exist at the highest level of Heaven. When God looked away from the crucifixion, the evil spirits openly cursed God. They believed that Jesus was a mere human. They had always been able to conceal their hatred of God, but unbeknownst to Satan, Jesus is God. Jesus is now a witness against the devil.

This is how God destroys evil, and this is the real reason Jesus suffered on the cross. The physical pain was nothing to God. The Lord is repulsed by evil. The Lord witnessed a supernatural expression of hatred, and by this He was tortured on the cross.

Even to this day, the devil does not know that Jesus is the Lord, and that Jesus is a witness against him.

At the crucifixion Jesus witnessed all the evil spirits' hatred of God, and by His testimony Jesus destroys all evil. This frees us from the dominion of Satan. The crucifixion is represented by the wine of the Last Supper, and it is represented by the blood that flowed from the side of Christ.

Freeing us from the dominion of Satan is essential to our redemption, but it does not erase our past sins. There is another crucial part of our redemption which is achieved by Christ giving up His body. The bread of the Last Supper represents the body of Christ that is given up for us. The water that flowed from His side represents separation by which we are redeemed. In the Bible water is often separated from water like when the children of Israel were delivered across the Red Sea. Water was parted when the children of Israel were brought across the Jordan River into the promised land.

Luke 22:19 And he took bread, and gave thanks, and brake it, and gave unto them, saying, This is my body which is given for you: this do in remembrance of me.

Our redemption is achieved by Jesus simply giving up His body (bread) like He said He would. Christ discards His body or separates (water) Himself from His body on the Day of Judgment.

Even the devil has acknowledged that Christ is fully human, but Christ is also sinless so His resurrection to eternal life is completely justified.

If God loves us, He must respect us. God will not rebuild us or alter us like toys, but Christ is one of us. If Christ discards His flesh, this justifies the discarding of our flesh on the Day of Judgment. Our sinless spirit is given a new body. The flesh is not evil, but as stated by Christ, the flesh is weak. The flesh is manipulated by spiritual forces, but while Satan causes our flesh to sin, our spirit is without sin.

Matthew 26:41 Watch and pray, that ye enter not into temptation: the spirit indeed is willing, but the flesh is weak.

This will redeem all children of God even those who do not believe in Jesus and those who have never heard of Jesus. The grace of Christ will make us worthy of eternal life. It will transform us into angels of God who are able to enjoy eternal life.

Our spirit is a small angel of God, perfect and without sin.

This is not Gnosticism; it merely has similarities to a non-blasphemous aspect of Gnosticism. The Gnostics did believe in a struggle between spirit and flesh which they saw as a struggle between good and evil, but it was other Gnostic beliefs that were blasphemous. Gnosticism was a remarkably effective distraction. Some of their beliefs were so blasphemous that for almost two thousand years Christians have vehemently opposed anything associated with Gnosticism.

There are many clues in the Bible to suggest that the struggle between good and evil is a struggle between spirit and flesh. The idea that we are redeemed by separation has incredible Biblical support. It is miraculous that people cannot see the great abundance of separation in the Bible.

Separation is everywhere in the Bible. Not just the parting of the Red Sea, redemption is compared to refining gold which is separating the gold. There are many ceremonies where blood, water, or oil is sprinkled. Circumcision is the act of separating flesh. The children of Israel were separated from the Egyptians. These are all acts of separation that are connected to redemption. Goats and sheep are said to be separated as are wheat and tares.

Jesus said if your eye causes you to sin, then pluck it out. The Lord does not want us to pluck out our eyes, He is giving a clue as to how He redeems us. If a person is part good and part evil, throw out the part that is evil and keep the part that is good.

God even created the world by separating things.

Genesis 1:4 And God saw the light, that it was good: and God divided the light from the darkness.

Genesis 1:6-7 And God said, Let there be a firmament in the midst of the waters, and let it divide the waters from the waters. And God made the firmament, and divided the waters which were under the firmament from the waters which were above the firmament: and it was so.

If Christians had recognized that Jesus redeems us by separating our spirit from our flesh, there would have been a lot of thought and discussion trying to find some other explanation for why Jesus suffered on the cross. Gnosticism had to be used as a distraction. Without Gnosticism, Christian scholars would surely realize that Jesus destroys the devil as a witness.

The Apocalypse or Revelation of the Messiah is when it is revealed in Heaven that Jesus transcends Heaven. This will lead to a war, or a debate between the archangel Michael and the devil. The devil will be cast from Heaven.

Jesus transcends Heaven, but this truth could not be revealed until the time of the end because this revelation causes the end. This is why Jesus spoke in riddles and this is why the Bible is enigmatic.

God had a reason to create evil, or to create the conditions where evil would form. Evil must be contained within time and ultimately destroyed. There will come a time when God destroys all evil, and that is called the Day of Judgment. Thanks to the testimony of Christ, the evil spirits will be destroyed on the Day of Judgment. We are part evil, and we must also be destroyed. Fortunately, Christ separates our spirit from our flesh making us worthy of eternal life in the kingdom of God.

Jesus saves us to eternal life on the Day of Judgment, however, there are many things from which a person can be saved. Our righteousness can save us here in this life. This is called temporal judgment, or punishment and reward before the Day of Judgment. God executes perfect justice, so all our sins will be required of us before the Day of Judgment.

The Day of Judgment is to destroy evil; it is not about executing measured justice. God punishes sin and rewards righteousness before the Day of Judgment. These are two completely different objectives.

Much of the confusion and debate concerning conflicting Biblical passages and doctrines can be solved by realizing that references to heaven, hell, salvation or being saved can sometimes be referring to temporal judgment before the Day of Judgment.

Some Biblical passages are referring to eternal life determined on the Day of Judgment, and some passages can be applied to both temporal judgment and eternal judgment.

In Judaism, the idea of resurrection and eternal life only appeared not long before Christ. Throughout the Old Testament, judgment and the Law referred to punishment or reward in this life. With Christianity this was somehow transformed into the idea that all references to judgment in the Bible are referring to eternal judgment.

Christians tend to believe that our actions in this life must have eternal consequences on the Day of Judgment, otherwise we have no incentive to lead a righteous life. Punishment can be extremely severe even if it is not eternal. Reward does not have to be eternal to be incredible. Jesus often said, "The kingdom of heaven is at hand", meaning heaven is here and now. Before the Day of Judgment, all righteousness will be rewarded, and all evil will be punished. Repentance can save us from temporal judgment. Only Jesus can save us on the Day of Judgment, and Jesus has already saved us without any help from us.

Christians often deal with conflicting Biblical doctrines by not taking passages literally even if the passage seems to be intended literally. Christians will endlessly argue over which passage to take literally and which passage to not take literally.

Most Christians do not take literally those parts of the Bible that indicate God predetermined who would go to Heaven. Nobody takes literally the Biblical claims that the children of God do not commit any sins. Christians completely avoid very clear statements in the Bible that

God will not punish anyone for the sins of someone else. Christians will struggle with passages that indicate we cannot lose our salvation. Everyone seems to avoid the Biblical statements that God created darkness and God created the wicked for the day of evil.

This theology explains why the Bible can say the children of God do not commit sin. The spirit of love within us is the real child of God made in the image of God. It does not commit any sin. This theology explains why the Bible can say we only make it to Heaven through Christ, yet we are judged by our works, or what we do, yet God predetermined who would go to Heaven, and no one is punished for the sins of someone else.

We only make it to Heaven through Christ, but our redemption is not achieved by Christ being punished for our sins. Since Jesus discards His flesh, it is perfectly reasonable for our flesh to be discarded. The perfect spirit of love within us came from God, and God predetermined who would be born with the spirit.

We will be judged by our words and actions, sometimes called our "works". On the Day of Judgment, our flesh will be judged by works and will be found unworthy. Our spirit will be judged by works and will be found worthy of eternal life in the kingdom of God. We cannot lose our eternal salvation since our spirit is perfect and without sin. While in the flesh, we can sin and suffer temporal judgment.

Evil is not the result of God giving us "free will" which somehow allows us to be both good and evil. As stated in the Bible, God formed darkness and God made the wicked for the day of evil. What we view as free will is a result of us being small angels of God attached to flesh. It is the flesh that is manipulated by evil spirits.

It is said that God would not create Satan as a loveless spirit and then punish Satan eternally for being evil. God had reasons to create the conditions where evil would form, and God will not eternally punish the loveless spirits He created. The devil is said to be tormented forever and ever. It is also said that time comes to an end. If time comes to an end, then forever and ever comes to an end.

The timeline we are on had a beginning, and it has an ending. Christ goes to prepare a place for us, so God will take us somewhere else, perhaps another timeline or another universe. Perhaps God has created an entirely different big bang. There is a new heaven and a new Earth. It is not clear what God will do with Satan at the end of the current timeline. God will deal with Satan and all evil spirits with perfect righteousness. Jesus said that God is kind to the unthankful and the evil.

Luke 6:35 But love ye your enemies, and do good, and lend, hoping for nothing again; and your reward shall be great, and ye shall be the children of the Highest: for he is kind unto the unthankful and to the evil.

This book has more Biblical support and takes the Bible more literally than what any church teaches. There is the Day of Judgment when God destroys evil, and there is temporal judgment where God executes justice. Understanding these two different objectives of judgment causes conflicting Biblical passages to be reconciled.

Christians do not seem to care that vicarious atonement is clearly rejected by the Scriptures. They have become accustomed to the Bible having some passages that clearly contradict their beliefs. They have become accustomed to saying, "it is a mystery", to having many questions that cannot be answered.

Christians have come to accept without examination the idea that the devil is powerful enough to do battle with God, and stupid enough to do battle with God. This theology presents a devil that is far more realistic and believable.

Satan causes us to sin while he stays within the Law. In the end, God turns the tables on Satan. Satan tried to show that power overcomes love, but God shows that love overcomes power.

This is something else that is accomplished by creation.

This theology is consistent with both the Jewish Scriptures and the Nicene Creed.

Chapter 3 – Jesus is Fully God

There were clues from the prophets that the Messiah would be Divine, but Jewish scholars rejected the Divinity of Jesus. To this day the Jews reject Jesus primarily because they reject the Divinity of a human. If Jesus is the Lord, all other objections to Him being the Messiah disappear. A Divine Jesus is still alive and can still fulfill all prophecies of the Messiah.

Matthew 16:15-16 He saith unto them, But whom say ye that I am? And Simon Peter answered and said, Thou art the Christ, the Son of the living God.

It was revealed to Peter that Jesus was the Son of God, but Peter did not take this title literally. After the death of Christ, Peter and the other apostles would not believe that Jesus had risen from the dead. It was only after meeting the resurrected Jesus that the apostles came to understand that Jesus is literally the Son of God.

Jewish scholars did not take Son of God literally, Peter did not take Son of God literally. When Satan tempted Christ, the devil did not take Son of God literally either. The idea that a human can be God is absurd. Because they believe that Jesus is Lord, Christians do not realize how hard it is to believe that a human can be God.

Even believing that Christ is Lord, Christians do not fully consider what it means that Jesus is the Lord. Being fully human does not require that Jesus forfeit any of His Divine power. Being fully God means that Jesus has all power and all knowledge. Even as a baby He could have caused the universe to disappear if He so desired.

Granted, Jesus could have suppressed any of His Divine power, but it would entirely be under His control.

Being fully God means that Jesus is absolute Righteousness.

Being fully human simply meant that He was attached to a human body and was born into this world. Fully human meant His body was fully part of Jesus. The humanity of Jesus was acknowledged by Satan and all the evil spirits when they cursed God at the crucifixion.

While He continued to exist at a level of reality that transcends Heaven, Jesus had a human body and a human soul. His body and soul were comparable to the body and soul of any human. Fully human meant that His emotions would be exposed by his body. Sorrow caused Jesus to weep, and the anguish of the cross caused Jesus to respond like a human in pain.

Christians believe that Jesus fully experienced what it means to be human when He walked the Earth, but that is not entirely possible. Jesus could not experience all the emotions, the ups and downs of human life when He walked the Earth, at least not within Himself. Jesus did not experience sorrow when someone died since the dead are safe in His hands. He experienced sorrow through others as He has experienced emotions through His children throughout time.

Jesus would have had no fear, and no worries (other than the cross). Jesus would know the thoughts of those around Him, repulsed by those who were selfish or angry, but able to be one with, and to feel the emotions of those experiencing righteous emotions.

Jesus fasted for forty days, but He could have fasted for any length of time.

Jesus was never tempted. Tempted by Satan does not mean that the Lord even for a moment gave any consideration to any offer the devil made. It is not necessary that Jesus was ever tempted for Him to be fully human.

Isaiah 55:9 For as the heavens are higher than the earth, so are my ways higher than your ways, and my thoughts than your thoughts.

It is not only God the Father who thoughts are beyond our comprehension, this is also true of God the Son. While He walked the Earth, it is likely true that His attention was focused on the physical location of His body, but Jesus can have a conversation with everyone in the world at the same time. His righteousness and His power are both unlimited.

When He said He would be with us to the end of the world, He was talking about all His children. He has been with, and He will be with all His children throughout the world. Not just in our presence but often within our souls. When we are righteous, He is within us.

Matthew 28:20 Teaching them to observe all things whatsoever I have commanded you: and, lo, I am with you always, even unto the end of the world. Amen.

Jesus greatly transcends the angels and all the spirit world, and He would certainly be able to hide His Divinity from any human or spirit.

Matthew 8:28-29 And when he was come to the other side into the country of the Gergesenes, there met him two possessed with devils, coming out of the tombs, exceeding fierce, so that no man might pass by that way. And, behold, they cried out, saying, What have we to do with thee, Jesus, thou Son of God? art thou come hither to torment us before the time?

If any demon knew that Jesus was Lord, it would only be because Jesus revealed Himself to that demon. He could just as easily make the demon forget that He is Lord.

Christians assume that the spirits of Heaven must all know that Jesus is God. After all, the inhabitants of Heaven must know that the Trinity is true.

> *James 2:19 Thou believest that there is one God; thou doest well: the devils also believe, and tremble.*

The devils know that God exists, the devils fear God, but that does not mean they know that Jesus is the Son of God. God is in Heaven, but God also transcends Heaven. That would be God the Holy Spirit in Heaven and God the Father transcending Heaven. The inhabitants of Heaven would likely recognize this as one God.

No matter how firmly Christians believe that Jesus is the Lord, an arrogant egocentric spirit like Satan is not going to seriously entertain the idea that a puny little human could be greater than him. It must be shown in Heaven that Jesus is the Son of God, and that has not happened yet.

Christ is the Lord and was able to witness the devil's hatred of God, but to this day, only Christians believe that Jesus is Lord. Jesus is at the right hand of God, a place that transcends Heaven. The inhabitants of Heaven would not necessarily know that Jesus is even still alive.

Chapter 4 – The Reason God Created the World

It is taken for granted that God created the world as a trial or a test. God gave us free will, and God will judge us on the Day of Judgment. Jesus had to die for our sins because we could not pass the test, so creation must be a test. Creation as a test also provides an explanation for the existence of evil. God gives us free will so we can choose to be good or evil, we can choose to be with God or to reject God. Free will results in evil as a free choice that people sometimes make.

It is believed that all who are judged by God must be freely able to choose between good and evil. God would not make Satan evil and then punish Satan for being evil. Angels and demons are believed to have been completely the same when they were created. Angels made the choice to be with God, while demons made the choice to reject God. That free choice would determine their nature.

Humans on the other hand are given a whole lifetime to make their choice, and religious scholars disagree on how humans and their choices will be judged. While the details may vary, we will be judged on the Day of Judgment, so creation is believed to be a test.

Christians believe that God punished Christ for our sins, but this means that Christ passes the test for us. The whole point of creation was to see who could pass a test. Then God passes those who failed the test if they admit that they failed the test. So, creation is a test to see who accepts Jesus, or who makes the choice to be with God regardless of how righteous they were in life.

People who never heard of Christ, and those who lived before Christ have the disadvantage of having to comply with the Law of God. God waited four thousand years into creation to provide some people with a shortcut. That shortcut would make eternal life in Heaven far easier to obtain.

This seems incredibly unfair, and yet it is universally agreed without question that creation is a test. Even people who believe in predestination believe that creation is a test because of the Day of Judgment. It is taken for granted that creation is a test. Those who fail this test will be tormented, destroyed, or live forever in a miserable existence separated from God.

An honest examination of the universe makes it clear that God has incredible power and intelligence, far beyond our ability to comprehend. The God of the Bible transcends time. If God was conducting a test, if that was the very purpose of creation, then surely, God could have designed a much better test.

If God wanted to see who would freely decide to be with Him, He could have designed a perfectly fair test. God could have put billions of people through a simulation of some kind. God could have designed a simulation where everyone had an equal chance of making the right choices. Regardless of the criteria of judgment, be it achieving a level of goodness or choosing to be with God, the world is an extremely unlevel playing field.

God created a world where people live in many different environments and have profoundly different influences. The information that is available to people will also vary to a massive degree. In their lifetime people are exposed to a wide variety of ideas, associations, hardships, and handicaps. People are from different nations, religions, time periods, social classes, and economic levels, from kings to slaves.

God can make allowances for those He knows in His infinite wisdom would have made better choices if not for one thing or another. If God makes any such allowances, then creation is not a test.

God in His infinite wisdom may know all the souls who would have made the right choice under the right circumstances. If He takes those people to Heaven on that basis then God would be taking people to Heaven based on their nature. No regard would be given to what they did in life. There would be no point in giving a test, to throw out the results and judge everyone based on their nature.

God may judge us based on our nature, but if He does, then creation is not a test.

Another problem with the idea that creation is a test is that we do not all have the same nature. It is not only our environment that varies greatly, but also the nature we are born with. Two people can experience a very similar environment and turn out radically different. It would have to be true that people are different by nature.

There are some people who are more loving, and there are some people who are more selfish. We were not all created with the same level of righteousness, and there may be some people completely void of righteousness.

Since humans were not all created with the same nature, this is also likely true for spirits as well. Angels are angels because God made them as loving spirits. Demons are demons because God did not make them as loving spirits and they became evil. Even if they were not given righteousness, it is still justice for demons to be punished for suffering they cause, but demons usually do not cause any suffering as they know they will be punished.

We see this with many strange supernatural creatures that humans have encountered. People have encountered many creatures that are scary but usually cause no harm. Demons are not allowed to kill people, otherwise humanity would not survive.

Demons may openly curse God, for which they are cast out of Heaven. Their hatred will make them unworthy on the Day of Judgment, but hatred that is not acted upon does not result in punishment in temporal judgment.

Giving righteousness to angels and not to demons is unfair if creation is a test. If creation is not a test, fairness is not an issue.

If God did not give Satan any righteousness so that Satan became evil, God might still punish Satan. The devil can fairly be punished for suffering that he causes, but the devil usually does not directly cause any suffering. Satan influences humans who cause suffering. As far as the Day of Judgment, the devil is condemned by his hatred of God, but we cannot really know what God will do with Satan. The only passage in the Bible that seems to clearly support a place of eternal torment is not as clear as it seems.

Revelation 20:10 And the devil that deceived them was cast into the lake of fire and brimstone, where the beast and the false prophet are, and shall be tormented day and night for ever and ever.

The original text could be translated as, "unto the ages of the ages", which has to do with time. This same book of Revelation says that time will end.

Revelation 10:6 And sware by him that liveth for ever and ever, who created heaven, and the things that therein are, and the earth, and the things that therein are, and the sea, and the things which are therein, that there should be time no longer:

Time has a beginning, and time has an ending. This means our eternal life in the kingdom of God could be on another timeline. Anything that is said to last forever could be everlasting on the current timeline which comes to an end.

Luke 6:35 But love ye your enemies, and do good, and lend, hoping for nothing again; and your reward shall be great, and ye shall be the children of the Highest: for he is kind unto the unthankful and to the evil.

At the crucifixion the Lord confronted evil, and the Lord has a full understanding of evil. Perhaps the devil needs to be destroyed for his own sake. Whatever God decides to do with Satan will be perfect righteousness.

God created many loving angels. Some of them were attached to fleshly bodies and born into this world. God will provide eternal life for all His angels. God created some spirits that were not given righteousness. They became evil, but we do not know what God will do with them. From puppies to Archangels, God did not create equality of power or equality of righteousness. There is nothing unfair about this if creation is not a test.

Proverbs 16:4 The Lord hath made all things for himself: yea, even the wicked for the day of evil.

Isaiah 45:6-7 That they may know from the rising of the sun, and from the west, that there is none beside me. I am the Lord, and there is none else. I form the light, and create darkness: I make peace, and create evil: I the Lord do all these things. Drop down, ye heavens, from above, and let the skies pour down righteousness: let the earth open, and let them bring forth salvation, and let righteousness spring up together; I the Lord have created it. Woe unto him that striveth with his Maker! Let the potsherd strive with the potsherds of the earth. Shall the clay say to him that fashioneth it, What makest thou? or thy work, He hath no hands?

There is a Day of Judgment, but the world was not created for the purpose of judgment.

Since God did not create the world as a test, there would have to be some other reason for God to have created the world. A loving

God would certainly want to create others outside of Himself to have someone to love, but God could have simply created loving angels in a world without evil or death.

Since God transcends time, creation would have to be an inherent and unavoidable product of the essence of God. Creation must provide something to God that is essential to the essence of God. What creation provides to God is something that was always part of God as creation is something that is always in the face of God.

It would have to be true that God created the world for His own purpose. God did not create the world for our benefit as we are an effect, not the cause. Just as people once believed the sun rotates the Earth, we have always tended to believe creation is about us. Creation is not about us; it is about God. If God created the world to have someone to love, creation is about God and His need to have someone to love. It is not about those He created to love. It would have to be true that the essence of God requires having someone to love.

God did not create the world so that we might gain knowledge or wisdom by our experiences in the world. God could have created us with any wisdom or knowledge that He wanted us to have if God possessed that wisdom to be able to give it to us.

Surely God has all wisdom, but some wisdom could not possibly exist without creation. Without creation God would have no understanding of sorrow, loneliness, or many other emotions. God could not give us any knowledge or wisdom that God did not possess. It seems ridiculous to suggest that God might not have this wisdom. It seems ridiculous to suggest that there could be any knowledge or wisdom that God does not possess. Surely, God has all wisdom, but the essentialness of wisdom is why creation exists.

Emotions cannot be calculated; they must be experienced. While God may eternally possess the wisdom of the human experience, it must be true that there is a human experience. A world of conflict between good and evil must exist contained within the borders of time for the wisdom gained by creation to be part of God.

God watches over us, sometimes from a distance. We are repulsive to God when we are angry or selfish. When we are contrite or sorrowful, God is not merely with us, God is inside us, even within our mind and soul. In our most difficult times, God feels precisely what we feel. God experiences our feelings. God has felt the sorrow, loneliness, and anxiety of all His children throughout time. Because of this, God has a full understanding of love. God has wisdom that is essential to His essence by sharing the journey of life with billions of His children.

The essence of God is absolute and infinite righteousness. Creation is the natural and unavoidable product of a loving God. A loving God would want to experience emotions that God experiences through us. It would be essential for a loving God to know what exactly love is.

Considering the purpose of creation, unfairness was unavoidable.

In an army there are many different units. There is infantry, artillery, communications, supply, and many other specialties. During a war the hardships and death will vary greatly among the different units. It is not fair, but it is unavoidable because there are different weapons and different missions. The purpose of the army is to win the war, which is essential.

The purpose of creation requires that God leave us in the dark. If we do not know what happens to our departed loved ones, we experience sorrow. There needed to be waves of generations, many people over a long period of time, growing more distant from God, spread out over a large world. Over time different societies would be shaped by different ideologies. Some societies would be influenced by ideologies by which they are more violent. Some societies would be influenced by ideologies by which they are more prosperous.

As humans commit evil and cause suffering, it is inevitable that some people will experience more suffering than others. Some people live in a time of peace, and other people live in a time of war.

God will repay, and God will judge fairly, but some will sin more because of the hardship of their life or the ideology of their society. It is not fair, but it is unavoidable considering the purpose of creation.

The world is an unlevel playing field not because that is a requirement considering the purpose of creation, but because that is unavoidable result considering the purpose of creation.

The purpose of creation is not the struggle between good and evil, but the results of that struggle.

The world may look like a test, but if you look more closely, it looks more like a journey or a story. Stories are all around us. These stories are filled with emotions that define love. We can see that the purpose of our world is the journey of life if we take a good look at the journey of life. God sends us on this journey for God to share the journey with us.

We can see the importance of family in the Bible, and the importance of family values. God did establish the family from the beginning and God put great emphasis on the family. Marriage and children are essential in our journey. Without marriage and children there is no journey of life, but it is the journey itself that is so remarkable.

Young people fall in love. They get married and have children. They experience many ups and downs and a wide variety of emotions. Sometimes a spouse dies, and sometimes a child dies. Sometimes they grow old together and watch their children go out and take the same journey. This is the world God created. It does appear to be a test, but it looks more like a journey with many hills and valleys.

There are many stories that have been told throughout human history. Stories of tragedy, stories of sacrifice and heroism, stories of loyalty and betrayal. Every story imaginable, and millions of stories that no human writer could ever imagine. God has experienced every moment of every human story.

Consider the harm that is done to a person who is isolated, how humans are not made to be alone. We need to have other people in our life, and each relationship is a story being told. Also consider the importance of storytelling, how even Jesus communicated in parables. The Bible is a collection of books filled with stories. Wisdom and knowledge are communicated in stories.

The human experience has included a great deal of suffering.

Many modern people live a comfortable life, but throughout history most people have experienced a harsh environment, socially, economically, and physically. Most people have been subjugated to some degree, often with great violence.

There has been war, famine, genocide, and slavery. But even people who lived in extreme difficulty have experienced more joy than we may realize. Marriage and childbirth, and time with friends and family would be more precious and more appreciated by people who lived a hard life. Still, it has often been wondered why God allows suffering, but there would have to be suffering if suffering is the whole point of creation.

There are two types of suffering. There is personal suffering, and there is the emotional pain of watching the suffering of someone you love. For example, there is the child who dies a painful death from cancer, and there is the mother who watches her child die. God is with the child, and we do not actually know how much the child suffered.

As far as the suffering of the mother is concerned, the world was created for the suffering of the mother. It is inconceivable that a grieving mother who watched her child die, could one day stand before God, the Foundation of all existence, and the omniscient God might not understand her pain.

It is inconceivable that a loving God could not understand what her heartache feels like, but God does fully understand her heartache because He has experienced it millions of times. He has experienced it personally and has felt the same pain that every grieving mother has felt. We cannot comprehend the great sorrow that the Lord has felt. God has felt all the sorrow of all His children throughout history.

God must experience sorrow through us. He cannot grieve for those who die, since He knows that death is defeated. This can be seen in the gospel of John when Jesus raised Lazarus from the dead.

Before Jesus went to Bethany, He knew Lazarus was dead, but He first told His disciples that Lazarus was sleeping. Jesus views death as being asleep. There is no indication that Jesus was bothered by the death of Lazarus. Jesus knows with complete certainty that death is nothing. Lazarus was completely safe in the hands of Jesus Himself. There would be no reason for Jesus to feel any sorrow for Lazarus. Jesus wept when He saw Mary, but Jesus did not merely see Mary. He saw her soul. He felt her sorrow.

John 11:33-35 When Jesus therefore saw her weeping, and the Jews also weeping which came with her, he groaned in the spirit, and was troubled. And said, Where have ye laid him? They said unto him, Lord, come and see. Jesus wept.

Jesus was not weeping for Lazarus; He was weeping for Mary.

God did not create the world for us to suffer, but for God to suffer. It was not for us to experience sorrow and loneliness, but for God to experience sorrow and loneliness through us.

The purpose of creation is for God to experience and know the emotions of our journey in life. Even with that purpose God could have created a type of simulation where evil and death are not real. God could have had real people going through a simulation causing them to experience real emotions.

If God had created a simulation where evil is not real, He could still have real humans experiencing real emotions in a simulated world, but God would be making no sacrifice Himself, other than sharing our pain. God would also be showing no respect to us. We would be mere tools. By creating a world where evil and judgment are real, God is acknowledging our existence. This is essential if God truly loves us.

Ephesians 6:9 And, ye masters, do the same things unto them, forbearing threatening: knowing that your Master also is in heaven; neither is there respect of persons with him.

We are almost never viewed as the slaves of God in the Bible. When we are described as slaves, it is only rhetorical. We are not the slaves of God; we are the children of God. If God had created a simulation where evil is not real, we would be like tools. We would be like objects or slaves.

By creating a world where evil is real, God is saying we are not tools. By creating a world where evil is real and God pays a price to destroy evil, God is saying we are His children.

Instead of a simulation, God created a world where evil is real, death is real, and there is a Day of Judgment. In all these things God acknowledges that we are His children. God acknowledges our existence. This is a commitment to us. We exist because God says we exist. This is significant since God is really all that exists. Everything else that exists only exists at the good pleasure of God. God is the foundation of all existence. God is the dreamer, but we are merely the dream. Can the dream go somewhere and build a life for itself without the dreamer?

God not only experiences all the sorrow that all His children have experienced, but God also created the world in a way that would cause Him far greater suffering than we can comprehend to redeem us. That suffering occurred at the crucifixion. Jesus is a witness against the devil and His testimony will destroy the devil. Jesus frees us from the dominion of Satan. The Lord is repulsed by evil, and we cannot begin to understand the incredible agony of the Lord when all the hatred of the demonic spirits was poured out on Him when He was crucified.

If God had destroyed evil a long time ago, we would not be here. God created existence outside of Himself and He gave free agency to various entities outside of Himself. Because of actions taken by Satan and our ancestors, we exist. Because of actions taken by humans, and malicious spiritual forces there is sin and there is suffering. It is obviously true that God foreknew there would be suffering. God created the conditions where there would be suffering, but that was the whole point of creation.

To say that God does not cause our suffering is not to deny that God executes justice. God created everything, and God is perfect righteousness. God must respond to suffering. God had a reason to create the conditions where evil would form, but evil must be contained within time and ultimately destroyed. That is the Day of Judgment. Those who cause suffering should experience the suffering they cause. That is temporal judgment.

God may love a person who has committed murder, but He also loves the murder victim, so the murderer must pay a heavy price.

Some people experience suffering greater than their sins, but God did not cause their suffering. Suffering is usually caused by natural forces or human evil. In executing justice, God would not cause suffering greater than what someone deserves. If someone suffers more than they deserve, that suffering would not have come from God. It may be true that God allowed it, and that God foreknew it, but God did not cause it. God will repay those who suffered more than they deserved.

Some people have experienced anguish that is unimaginable. Like a mother who watches enemy soldiers kill her child. As is always the case when one of His children is in sorrow, God is with the mother. He feels what she feels. If her pain is too much for her to endure, God may cause her to lose consciousness.

Since God created the world to experience painful emotions, God will have gratitude for those through whom He experiences heartache. We know that God will balance all books. God will repay, and God will keep His word. God created the world in a way that demonstrates His commitment to us.

Evil is real, and judgment is real. God acknowledges our existence and God respects our existence. God will not change us, rebuild us, or manipulate us like toys. For this reason, God must justify the discarding of our flesh. By becoming human, and discarding His flesh, it is completely fair and reasonable that our flesh is discarded. God is not changing us without justification because He acknowledges and respects our existence. We have assurance that God will never change us in some way and throw us out of Heaven.

With the design of creation, God is expressing His commitment to us, and His love for us. God is committed to us, and God is grateful to us. We provide something to God that the angels in Heaven cannot provide. We pay a price to provide God with wisdom that is essential to God, so God paid an enormous price for us.

Creation is not a test to see who accepts Jesus, but a journey through a world of joy and suffering to provide an understanding of what love is. Creation provides God with an understanding of who God is. Our decisions can determine how difficult this journey is, but our redemption to eternal life is not a result of our decisions. God will redeem all His children. Notwithstanding, God did create spirits who lack the ability to love, and this could be true of some humans as well. The purpose for creation does not prevent God from redeeming all His children therefore God will devise a way to achieve that goal, yet God must justify everything He does.

Chapter 5 – The Separation of Spirit and Flesh

When He came into Jerusalem many people believed that Jesus was the Messiah. The timing seemed to be right based on a prophecy of Daniel. John the Baptist was seen as a prophet, and he seemed to be announcing the imminent arrival of the Messiah. Some people were still alive who remembered the visit by the Magi. Jesus was performing great miracles.

There was even an earthquake and darkness when Jesus was crucified, and yet shortly thereafter, not many Jews accepted Jesus as the Messiah. Jesus failed to do what the Messiah was expected to do. Most significantly Jesus did not establish His kingdom. The death of Christ would convince everyone that Jesus could never establish His kingdom. Jesus could never fulfill all the other prophecies of the Messiah because He was dead.

On the cross, Jesus did establish His kingdom in the world to come. The kingdom of the Messiah on Earth is yet to come, but the Jews were not looking for a Messiah to establish a kingdom in the world to come. The Jews who witnessed the resurrected Jesus were believers, even if they did not fully understand the purpose of His death and resurrection. Jews who did not have some miraculous experience would naturally reject the idea that Jesus was the Messiah.

Christianity was soon taken over by the gentiles because the gentiles did not have preexisting expectations of the Messiah. There are clues in the Scriptures that the Messiah might be Divine. This meant Jesus could return and fulfill all other prophecies sometime in the future.

The problem for the Jews was not that they failed to notice the clues of the Messiah's Divinity, but that they had had many centuries to interpret the coming of Messiah. They had already worked out their view of Messiah. The Jewish view of Messiah did not include the idea that He would be Divine. It does seem absurd that a man can be Divine, but God can do whatever He wants.

What the Christians had difficulty in explaining is how is Jesus Divine? What is the Trinity and why did Christ have to suffer? How are we redeemed by His suffering?

Originally most discussion about atonement was centered on Christ destroying Satan or Christ freeing us from the dominion of Satan. In some Orthodox churches it is still believed that Christ goes to the realm of death to rescue humanity. It is said that Christ descended into death to retrieve the keys of death. These original atonement theories did not provide details. It was not clear how Christ defeats the devil or how He rescues us by descending into the realm of death.

There was some discussion of Christ being punished for our sins, but such discussion was not as common. Christ as a substitute was discussed by church fathers who on other occasions would speak of Christ paying a ransom. This suggests that such statements were only rhetorical.

The most common view in the early church was that Christ destroys Satan, or Christ frees us from the dominion of Satan. We know this to be the case as the ransom theory would become the dominate theory of atonement. For the first thousand years of Christianity, the ransom theory was the most common answer to the question of how we are redeemed by Christ.

Mark 10:45 For even the Son of man came not to be ministered unto, but to minister, and to give his life a ransom for many.

The word ransom is associated with our redemption, but a ransom is a payment to set someone free. It does not make sense that the Lord had to make any type of payment to the devil. It also seems odd that God could not simply take the keys of death away from the devil.

The material world is the dominion of Satan, but this does not mean that the devil has leverage over God. The devil has ownership over us. The devil influences our flesh causing us to sin. We are tied to our fleshly bodies that the devil has corrupted.

The ransom theory was not the means of our atonement, but only the explanation for the means. Over a thousand years after Christ, led by the theologian Saint Anselm, the Church rejected the ransom theory. It also rejected the means of atonement which the ransom theory tried to explain. The Church embraced a brand-new means of our atonement, rejecting a thousand years of Church tradition.

What replaced the ransom theory was the satisfaction theory for Catholicism. This would eventually develop into penal substitutionary atonement for protestants. These two theories are very similar. Both are founded upon the idea that the suffering of Christ pays or provides penance for our sins, or otherwise satisfies our sins. Going forward they will both be called vicarious atonement.

One obvious weakness with both theories is that they are new. If true, vicarious atonement must have been revealed by the Holy Spirit. If revealed by the Holy Spirit, vicarious atonement was revealed a long time after Christ.

If the Holy Spirit waited for centuries to reveal information, then any theory revealed in the eleventh or sixteenth century would have no more credibility than a theory revealed in the twenty-first century. A theory revealed at the time of the end would be more credible. There might be a reason for some information to be revealed at that time. A revelation that occurs in the middle of the Church age seems less likely to be true.

The biggest problem with vicarious atonement is that it clearly contradicts the Scriptures. God does not punish anyone for the sins of someone else.

Proponents of vicarious atonement will sometimes say that God had a moral dilemma. Like someone who has promised to deliver a rich man's gold coins, but later encounters a hungry family. They can be honest and deliver the gold, or they can be compassionate and give a gold coin to the hungry family. God can do justice and punish us for our sins, or God can be merciful and punish Christ for our sin.

God is infinitely just, and infinitely merciful, but God is also infinitely intelligent. God cannot be lacking in His justice, or His mercy to the slightest degree. In his infinite intelligence, God will find a way to redeem us that does not require any injustice.

Vicarious atonement comes with variations in rhetoric, but it always claims that the righteousness or suffering of Christ is somehow applied to us. Vicarious atonement is a fundamental belief to many Christians. To reject vicarious atonement can be viewed by many as heresy.

It should be realized that for the first one thousand years after Christ, Christians did not believe in vicarious atonement. Christians also fail to consider the injustice of vicarious atonement.

If a convicted murderer is sentenced to execution, but an innocent volunteer offers to be executed instead of the murderer, no judge would accept the offer. If a judge were to accept the offer, then it could the said that the volunteer saved the murderer by taking his punishment. This is vicarious atonement. It could also be said that the judge is a horrible judge and should be removed from the bench. The court would be committing murder by killing an innocent volunteer.

There are many ways one person can pay the price for the actions of someone else. A person who is killed by a drunk driver could be said to have paid the price for the actions of the drunk driver.

Isaiah 53:5-6 But he was wounded for our transgressions, he was bruised for our iniquities: the chastisement of our peace was upon him; and with his stripes we are healed. All we like sheep have gone astray; we have turned every one to his own way; and the Lord hath laid on him the iniquity of us all.

According to the book of Isaiah, The Messiah died "for" our sins. He died "because" of our sins. By His stripes we are healed. This does not mean that He heals us by taking upon Himself the punishment for our sins. If our iniquity is "laid" on Him, that could mean He paid the price for our sins, but not necessarily by taking the punishment for our sins or by offering a penance for our sins.

There are numerous verses in the Bible that indicate Christ paid the price for our sins, They do not clearly indicate how the price was paid. The Messiah "heals" us, and He suffers because of our sins. It is not necessarily true that His suffering is what heals us. It is not necessarily true that He heals us by taking the punishment for our sins.

The problem with the ransom theory is that the devil does not have any leverage over God. If the ransom theory were true, then Christ would be redeeming us by paying a ransom to the devil. It would still be true that we are redeemed because of His suffering. It would still be true that He was wounded for our transgressions if He was paying a ransom. Jesus paying the price for our sins does not require that He takes the punishment for our sins.

It cannot be true that Jesus is taking the punishment for our sins. God is a just God, and according to the Bible, everyone will be accountable for their own sins.

Ezekiel 18:20 The soul that sinneth, it shall die. The son shall not bear the iniquity of the father, neither shall the father bear the iniquity of the son: the righteousness of the righteous shall be upon him, and the wickedness of the wicked shall be upon him.

If vicarious atonement is the true way in which God redeems His children, there should be significant Biblical support. Among all the stories of the Old Testament there should be stories where someone is punished for the sins of someone else. Such stories are difficult to find in the Bible. There were occasions when the nation was punished because of the wickedness of the king, but a righteous king was not punished for the wickedness of the people.

There are rare cases of substitution in the Bible. A ram was provided so Abraham did not have to sacrifice his son.

Abraham was told that the world would be blessed by his seed. This promise along with God asking Abraham to sacrifice his son points to Christ who is sacrificed. There is no clear indication in this story as to how the sacrifice of Christ redeems us. Abraham demonstrated faith, and the Messiah would come through his seed because of his faith. Abraham is not redeemed by his faith, but by the Messiah.

Moses offered to pay for the sins of the people. God rejected that offer and stated that everyone would pay for their own sin.

Exodus 32:31-33 And Moses returned unto the Lord, and said, Oh, this people have sinned a great sin, and have made them gods of gold. Yet now, if thou wilt forgive their sin—; and if not, blot me, I pray thee, out of thy book which thou hast written. And the Lord said unto Moses, Whosoever hath sinned against me, him will I blot out of my book.

In the following passage it is said that He bears our sin. To bear our sins does suggest paying the price, but that does not mean that He takes the responsibility for our sins.

Hebrews 9:27-28 And as it is appointed unto men once to die, but after this the judgment: So Christ was once offered to bear the sins of many; and unto them that look for him shall he appear the second time without sin unto salvation.

This next verse should not be taken literally. Christ did not literally become sin. This is rhetorical.

2 Corinthians 5:21 For he hath made him to be sin for us, who knew no sin; that we might be made the righteousness of God in him.

There are numerous passages in the Bible that clearly say everyone will pay for their own sins. These passages are often written in a way that seems undeniably literal.

If a passage seems literal, then we should try to take it literally. If the wording suggests that a passage is not literal, then we do not have to take it literally. Christian will read that everyone will pay for their own sins and say it should not be taken literally. They will read that Christ became sin and they will take it literally.

1 Peter 2:24 Who his own self bare our sins in his own body on the tree, that we, being dead to sins, should live unto righteousness: by whose stripes ye were healed.

We are not literally dead to sin, not yet. The spirit within us is without sin and we shall live unto righteousness in the world to come because of the suffering of Christ. Our sins are in His body figuratively, so that as Christ discards His body, our body and our sins are discarded.

Christ suffering to take our punishment or to somehow satisfy the justice or honor of God is not Biblical. There is no passage in the Bible that clearly communicates vicarious atonement.

There are no parables of Christ about one person becoming responsible for the sins of someone else. There are several passages in the Bible which allegedly support vicarious atonement, but almost all of them do not actually support it. The few passages that do support vicarious atonement seem to be figurative and not literal.

The idea that God punishes anyone for the sins of someone else contradicts clear text in the Bible. It conflicts with the idea of a just God which is abundantly supported by the Bible.

Vicarious atonement also conflicts with the Law of God we have written on our hearts. Granted, our experiences in life can modify our understanding of morality and ethics to some degree. Even if it may become blurry, every child of God knows the difference between right and wrong.

This is perhaps the best way to know that you are a child of God. You are a child of God because you have the Law of God written on your heart. We know that murder is wrong. Bearing false witness is wrong. We are a child of God if we are genuinely against evil, even evil within ourselves. We know it is wrong for Jesus, or anyone else, to suffer for what we have done.

The Son of God defeats the devil. This is best explained by understanding that God really did forsake Christ. When God looked away from the crucifixion, the devil believed he could safely curse God.

Jesus is at the Right Hand of God, a secret place that transcends Heaven. Satan did not know that Jesus is Divine. Christ is a witness against the devil and Christ destroys the devil. Destroying the devil frees us from the dominion of Satan, so that we can be without sin going forward.

All atonement theories focus entirely on how we are redeemed by Christ. The debate is about how our past sins are removed by Christ.

Little consideration is given to how the grace of Christ causes us to be perfect going forward.

It makes no sense for our redemption to only forgive or erase our past sins if we continue to sin. If we continue to sin, then we continue to need redemption. In the world to come, we must be transformed into children of God who do not sin. We can never achieve perfection, so the grace of Christ must somehow cause us to be perfect.

Destroying the devil will cause us to be sinless going forward if the influence of the devil is the cause of our sins. Destroying the devil does not erase the sins we have already committed. The grace of Christ should also remove our past sins. It should do this without unjustly transferring responsibility for our sins to Christ.

Ideally, our sins should not merely be forgiven, they should be made to no longer exist. Only then do we truly deserve to enter the kingdom of God.

> *John 1:29 The next day John seeth Jesus coming unto him, and saith, Behold the Lamb of God, which taketh away the sin of the world.*

Our sins are taken away.

It is commonly believed that we will have a new body in the resurrection. This new body could explain how we are made perfect in the kingdom of God. If we are without sin in our new body that means our new body and our spirit that occupies our new body are both sinless.

> *1 Corinthians 15:42-44 So also is the resurrection of the dead. It is sown in corruption; it is raised in incorruption: It is sown in dishonour; it is raised in glory: it is sown in weakness; it is raised in power: It is sown a natural body; it is raised a spiritual body. There is a natural body, and there is a spiritual body.*

Philippians 3:21 Who shall change our vile body, that it may be fashioned like unto his glorious body, according to the working whereby he is able even to subdue all things unto himself.

If our spirit and soul are sinless in our new body, then our spirit is not the source of our sins. The spirit that occupies our present body is sinless. Our sin in the present world comes from our current physical body. Granted it may be because of the influence of evil spirits that our current body is corrupted.

The third chapter of John is quoted to support the belief that we must accept Jesus, but this passage is perhaps the best example in the gospels showing how the spirit is perfect, but sin comes from the flesh.

John 3:3-4 Jesus answered and said unto him, Verily, verily, I say unto thee, Except a man be born again, he cannot see the kingdom of God. Nicodemus saith unto him, How can a man be born when he is old? can he enter the second time into his mother's womb, and be born?

In modern times a person who has a life changing experience is said to be born again. Based on the response of Nicodemus, being born again seemed to have had no meaning to him. By saying we must be born again, Jesus did not necessarily mean we must have a life changing experience.

John 3:5-6 Jesus answered, Verily, verily, I say unto thee, Except a man be born of water and of the Spirit, he cannot enter into the kingdom of God. That which is born of the flesh is flesh; and that which is born of the Spirit is spirit.

We must have a second birth. That second birth is not necessarily a product of a decision on our part. It is not necessarily some change which occurs to us during our lifetime. We did not decide to be born of the flesh, and we do not decide to be born of the Spirit. The spirit is born into us when our flesh is born. There is a perfect spirit of love that is born into the heart of every child of God. That spirit is born of God, but the flesh is born of flesh.

John 3:7-8 Marvel not that I said unto thee, Ye must be born again. The wind bloweth where it listeth, and thou hearest the sound thereof, but canst not tell whence it cometh, and whither it goeth: so is every one that is born of the Spirit.

The spirit is like the wind. A person can feel the wind, and they can see the effects of the wind. They can hear the wind, but they cannot see the wind. Likewise, we can feel the spirit within ourselves, and we can see the effects of the spirit on others, but we cannot see the spirit. We cannot know if someone is a child of God, or if everyone is a child of God.

John 3:12 If I have told you earthly things, and ye believe not, how shall ye believe, if I tell you of heavenly things? And no man hath ascended up to heaven, but he that came down from heaven, even the Son of man which is in heaven.

What Jesus has been telling Nicodemus up to this point is earthly. Now Jesus is turning His attention to how to earn eternal life on the Day of Judgment. No one has ascended to Heaven, no one has earned admission into the eternal kingdom of God other than Christ.

John 3:16-18 For God so loved the world, that he gave his only begotten Son, that whosoever believeth in him should not perish, but have everlasting life. For God sent not his Son into the world to condemn the world; but that the world through him might be saved. He that believeth on him is not condemned: but he that believeth not is condemned already, because he hath not believed in the name of the only begotten Son of God.

We must believe in the name of the only begotten Son of God to enter the eternal kingdom of Heaven. The Lord has many names, but this is not about believing in any particular name of the Lord.

The word name in this passage could be changed to the word essence. Regardless of what a person's name is, regardless of the word that is recorded on their birth certificate, their "name" is their essence. A person must believe in the essence of God, which is Righteousness.

The spirit inside the heart of every child of God believes in righteousness. The spirit inside every child of God believes in the name of the only begotten Son of God. Even people who have never heard of Jesus can have a spirit within themselves that believes in the essence of God.

This is the difference between the good and evil spirits of Heaven. It is the difference between good and evil people in this world. Those who believe in the name of God, which is those who believe in the essence of God are good. Those who believe in love are the children of God. Evil sees no value in love, so it believes in power.

John 3:19-21 And this is the condemnation, that light is come into the world, and men loved darkness rather than light, because their deeds were evil. For every one that doeth evil hateth the light, neither cometh to the light, lest his deeds should be reproved. But he that doeth truth cometh to the light, that his deeds may be made manifest, that they are wrought in God.

Those who believe in the name of the Son of God are the ones who come to the light. Those who do not believe in the name of the Son of God hate the light. The chapter begins with flesh and spirit; the chapter ends with those who do evil and those who do truth. The flesh does evil, but the spirit does truth.

This is another indication that the children of God are perfect. Those who are not children of God are not capable of righteousness. This cannot be talking about two different groups of people. Jesus is once again indicating that some people are perfect. The spirit within us is perfect. The flesh is not evil, it commits acts of evil because of the influence of the devil. The flesh is not capable of true righteousness.

The flesh loves darkness. We find pleasure in degrading ourselves and others. Yet, we see ourselves as the center of the universe. We enjoy eating the flesh of animals.

We also hunger and thirst after righteousness, but that comes from our spirit. Our spirit cometh to the light, but our flesh loves darkness.

When Christ told a crowd at the temple that they were from beneath, He was talking about their flesh, not their spirit.

John 8:23 And he said unto them, Ye are from beneath; I am from above: ye are of this world; I am not of this world.

He had previously said that the flesh is born of the flesh and the spirit is born of the Spirit. The people in this crowd possessed a spirit that came from above, and a body that came from beneath. When Jesus said they came from beneath this indicates He was speaking to their body, not their spirit.

Jesus would shortly thereafter say that their father was the devil.

John 8:44 Ye are of your father the devil, and the lusts of your father ye will do. He was a murderer from the beginning, and abode not in the truth, because there is no truth in him. When he speaketh a lie, he speaketh of his own: for he is a liar, and the father of it.

Our spirit is a child of God, but our flesh is a child of the devil. We are born and come into existence in the material world. We are born because of the influence of the devil. Satan has dominion over the material world by a spirit of selfishness he brings into the world causing sin which is repulsive to God. This was a perversion of God's creation by which we exist. Satan believes he merely must cause the humans to sin while suppressing his own hostility at least until the Day of Judgment.

If our sin comes from our current physical body, then God can redeem us simply by discarding our current physical body and giving us the new perfect body. God keeps our soul and our spirit because our sin does not come from our spirit.

Our spirit is without sin. God must justify discarding our flesh. God must justify changing us in this way since God must respect any creature He creates. It is the devil that sees no value in a human soul. God sees value in all creatures. God respects us as separate beings, and He would have to justify any change to us. If God loves us, He must respect us.

When Christ discards His flesh that justifies the discarding of our flesh. Christ is one of us. God can make this change to us, causing us to be perfect, while still respecting us as individuals.

Our past sins are removed, and we are sinless going forward. This atonement theory explains not only how we are redeemed. It explains how we are transformed into the perfect angels we must become to enter the perfect kingdom of God.

Christ redeems us by the discarding of His flesh. Our spirit which has not committed any sins can enter the perfect kingdom of God. This atonement theory may be considered revolutionary, but unlike vicarious atonement, it dates to the earliest years of Christianity.

The early church believed in Christus victor. They believed that Christ redeems us by destroying the devil or freeing us from the dominion of Satan. Ransom theory became the dominant theory of atonement because it provided an explanation for how Christ frees us from Satan, although ransom theory was not a very good explanation. The flawed ransom theory would be replaced by vicarious atonement many centuries after Christ.

To say that Christ gives up His flesh to free us is consistent with Christus victor. Christ as a witness against the devil to destroy evil explains Christus victor perfectly. Christus victor dates to the very early church. This explanation for Christus victor is consistent with the views of the very early church. This atonement theory is more consistent with early church tradition than what the church teaches today. This atonement theory is the real, original, church tradition.

The Messiah suffered to expose the sin of Satan and all the evil spirits. This is an explanation for the suffering and death of the Messiah that does not contradict the Jewish Scriptures. The destruction of evil is part of our redemption, and it explains why the Scriptures foretold a Messiah who suffers for us. One way the Scriptures point to a suffering Messiah was the great abundance of animal sacrifice.

In animal sacrifice, the sacrifice takes away sin. It was not believed that the sacrificed animal became responsible for the sins of the human. Christians will point to animal sacrifice as support for vicarious atonement, but animal sacrifice merely points to the sacrifice of the Messiah.

Animal sacrifice was a prophecy of the Messiah. Animal sacrifice does not tell us how the sacrifice of Christ takes away our sins. The way in which we are redeemed by the Messiah should not contradict the Scriptures. We are told that justice is more acceptable to the Lord than sacrifice.

Proverbs 21:3 To do justice and judgment is more acceptable to the Lord than sacrifice.

It never made sense that a God of unimaginable Love would ask His children to wastefully kill helpless animals. We know that there is no actual forgiveness of sin or removal of sin in animal sacrifice. Yet there had to be a reason for the animal sacrifice. Animal sacrifice points to the death of Christ. The destruction of the flesh of the animal in a burnt offering shows how we are redeemed by Christ.

After being killed, the animal's flesh is destroyed as Christ is not merely crucified, He also gives up His body. This justifies our body being discarded or separated leaving our sinless spirit worthy of eternal life.

In the Passover the lamb's flesh is eaten, but eating is only a different manner of destruction. Eating is a type of destruction that provides life to the eater. This is like the Eucharist where Christ gives up His flesh to provide life to His children.

Like animal sacrifice, it seems odd that the Lord would ask us to eat His flesh but there is a message in the Eucharist. The Messiah gives up His flesh for us to have life. There are many Biblical clues that present either destruction of flesh or separation as the means of redemption.

This is not Gnosticism. The Gnostics tried to present their religion as a type of Christianity. They even hijacked many of the founders of Christianity with false gospels that were supposedly written by apostles of Christ. These false gospels supported Gnosticism.

The Gnostics believed in a conflict between spirit and flesh, but this was not the blasphemous aspect of their religion. Gnostics rejected the God of the Bible, often believing the God of the Bible to be evil. Gnosticism promoted ideas that are arrogant and blasphemous. For two thousand years Christianity has opposed anything associated with Gnosticism.

Christians believe in the Old Testament, but this does not make them Jews. To share some beliefs with Judaism does not make a person Jewish. To share one belief with the Gnostics does constitute Gnosticism. Gnosticism was a distraction, preventing Christians from seeing a better explanation for many Biblical passages. Gnosticism took focus away from the struggle within us between spirit and flesh. It prevented the inevitable recognition of the great abundance of separation in the Bible.

We are angels of God attached to flesh. Satan manipulates our flesh causing us to be unworthy to enter the kingdom of God. The Messiah justifies the discarding of our flesh transforming us to angels of God. This is not to say that we will be disembodied spirits, granted that might not be a bad thing. We will be given a glorious new body. This means our existence will be similar in at least in some ways to the present world. We will be without hostility, selfishness, or self-righteousness.

This is not to deny the resurrection of our flesh, but just because our flesh is resurrected does not mean our flesh is worthy to enter the kingdom of God. Our flesh will be found guilty on the Day of Judgment. Our spirit will be found innocent.

John 5:29 And shall come forth; they that have done good, unto the resurrection of life; and they that have done evil, unto the resurrection of damnation.

This also does not mean there are no consequences for sin. We will have difficulties in this life and perhaps in purgatory because of our sins. We will have happiness in this life and perhaps a reward after death because of our righteousness. Under God there is perfect justice but no amount of refinement in time will ever lead to our being perfect or worthy to enter the kingdom of God.

Our redemption by Christ causes us to be perfect. The spirit of love within us is perfect and is given a new body. This not only means that we will deserve eternal life, this perfection which we can never obtain except through Christ is also necessary for us to enjoy eternal life. Heaven must involve a change to us, not merely taking us to a different place. The Messiah justifies this change to us.

Chapter 6 – Separation in the Bible

It is miraculous that God was able to keep secret the real way in which Christ redeems His children. There is great Biblical support for the idea that redemption is achieved by separation. God even created the world by separating things.

On the first day of creation, God divided the light from the darkness:

Genesis 1:4 And God saw the light, that it was good: and God divided the light from the darkness.

On the second day of creation God divided waters from waters.

Genesis 1:6-7 And God said, Let there be a firmament in the midst of the waters, and let it divide the waters from the waters. And God made the firmament, and divided the waters which were under the firmament from the waters which were above the firmament: and it was so.

On the third day God gathered the water together separating it from the land:

Genesis 1:9-10 And God said, Let the waters under the heaven be gathered together unto one place, and let the dry land appear: and it was so. And God called the dry land Earth; and the gathering together of the waters called he Seas: and God saw that it was good.

On the fourth day God divided the day from the night.

Genesis 1:17-18 And God set them in the firmament of the heaven to give light upon the earth, And to rule over the day and over the night, and to divide the light from the darkness: and God saw that it was good.

On the last two days God created all the various life forms and God created Adam and Eve. The world itself, created in those first four days, was created by separation. There is a great abundance of separating in the Bible. Often it is separating something which is good from something which is bad or neutral.

Christ said He would give up His body. Christians have repeated this verse so many times, they read it without paying attention to what it says. Chris will not only die for us; He will also give up His body for us.

Luke 22:19 And he took bread, and gave thanks, and brake it, and gave unto them, saying, This is my body which is given for you: this do in remembrance of me.

After His resurrection Christ showed His disciples that He still had His fleshly body.

Luke 24:39-40 Behold my hands and my feet, that it is I myself: handle me, and see; for a spirit hath not flesh and bones, as ye see me have. And when he had thus spoken, he shewed them his hands and his feet.

Christ keeps His word which means at some point He will give up His body. Then it will be fair for us to give up our bodies.

Matthew 13:24-26 Another parable put he forth unto them, saying, The kingdom of heaven is likened unto a man which sowed good seed in his field: But while men slept, his enemy came and sowed tares among the wheat, and went his way. But when the blade was sprung up, and brought forth fruit, then appeared the tares also.

Matthew 13:30 Let both grow together until the harvest: and in the time of harvest I will say to the reapers, Gather ye together first the tares, and bind them in bundles to burn them: but gather the wheat into my barn.

When God created the world, it was good. Satan is the enemy who sowed the tares or sin in the world. The wheat is the spirit in the child of God, while the tares are the flesh. The tares cannot be removed without uprooting the wheat just as our spirit and flesh will both be destroyed without the grace of Christ. At the harvest the tares and wheat will be separated. The spirit and flesh will be separated on the Day of Judgment.

Once the children of God are separated from their flesh their spirits are found worthy of eternal life. The spirit is sometimes called a seed in the Bible. It is a seed of love planted by God in the hearts of His children.

> *1 John 3:9 Whosoever is born of God doth not commit sin; for his seed remaineth in him: and he cannot sin, because he is born of God.*

> *1 John 5:18 We know that whosoever is born of God sinneth not; but he that is begotten of God keepeth himself, and that wicked one toucheth him not.*

Like our Father, our spirit is perfect. Once the selfish part of us is discarded we will have perfect love for God and for each other. The Bible states clearly in several passages that the children of God are perfect and without sin.

> *Matthew 7:18 A good tree cannot bring forth evil fruit, neither can a corrupt tree bring forth good fruit.*

Christian will say that we are not perfect, but we are forgiven. Repentance or confession is said to wash away our sins, but Jesus used words that very clearly communicated that the children of God do not commit sins.

> *John 3:20-21 For every one that doeth evil hateth the light, neither cometh to the light, lest his deeds should be reproved. But he that doeth truth cometh to the light, that his deeds may be made manifest, that they are wrought in God.*

There is a spirit within us that is perfect and does not commit any sin.

Matthew 5: 48 Be ye therefore perfect, even as your Father which is in heaven is perfect.

It seems odd that Christ should tell us to be perfect since we cannot be perfect. The day will come when we are made perfect by Christ. The kingdom of God is perfection and all who enter must be perfect. Anyone who has ever committed a sin, anyone who can be selfish or hateful, or deceptive cannot enter the kingdom of God. Without Christ there is no way we can ever become perfect or erase the sins we have committed.

Luke 20:35-36 But they which shall be accounted worthy to obtain that world, and the resurrection from the dead, neither marry, nor are given in marriage: Neither can they die any more: for they are equal unto the angels; and are the children of God, being the children of the resurrection.

Those worthy to obtain that world are equal to angel because they are angels. The angels are sometimes called the children of God, and when we discard our flesh, we will be angels. Granted our spirit may be smaller than most angels, but that would make us little children of God.

Matthew 18:3 And said, Verily I say unto you, Except ye be converted, and become as little children, ye shall not enter into the kingdom of heaven.

We must become little children. We must become little angels.

Christ stated the necessity of separating the flesh from the spirit. Without this the whole person is not worthy of eternal life and is cast into hell.

Matthew 5:29-30 And if thy right eye offend thee, pluck it out, and cast it from thee: for it is profitable for thee that one of thy members should perish, and not that thy whole body should be cast into hell. And if thy right hand offend thee, cut it off, and cast it from thee: for it is profitable for thee that one of thy members should perish, and not that thy whole body should be cast into hell.

In this passage Christ is basically saying that if a person is part good and part evil, throw away the part that is evil and keep the part that is good.

Only because of Christ can sinners enter eternal Heaven. If a person possesses something inside themselves which is perfect, that something can be separated from their flesh. That spirit, combined with the inner self, results in a person who is completely perfect.

1 Corinthians 5:5 To deliver such an one unto Satan for the destruction of the flesh, that the spirit may be saved in the day of the Lord Jesus.

The spirit is unselfish love in the heart of all children of God. It comes from God. God is Love and all love comes from God. There is nothing a person can do to obtain that spirit. If a person does not already have that spirit, they will likely have no desire for it.

A child of God is someone who has this love in their heart. If we have love within us, we will have eternal life regardless of our religious beliefs. It is the love within us which comes from God and is the true child of God.

When the Bible talks of the righteous, those born of God, it is talking about the spirits inside the children of God. The wicked, the ungodly, is often referring to the flesh including the flesh of the children of God.

When Christ was crucified, the veil was rent or torn in two. This tearing of the veil eliminated what stood between the people and the Holy. The death of Christ eliminated what stood between the children of God and Heaven.

Matthew 27:51 And, behold, the veil of the temple was rent in twain from the top to the bottom; and the earth did quake, and the rocks rent;

The veil is torn into two pieces just as Christ will separate Himself from His flesh. The rocks also rent just as the children of God will also be separated from their flesh.

In the Passover the Jews were separated from the Egyptians. Israel as a nation was born in bondage. Israel was bonded to or a part of Egypt. The Israelites represented the spirit. The Egyptians represented the flesh in which the spirit is contained. By the Passover, Israel was set free. It was because of the blood of a sacrificed lamb that the Israelites were "passed over" by death. The spirits in the children of God will escape death due to the sacrifice of the Messiah.

When the waters of the Red Sea were parted all the Israelites survived and all the Egyptians were destroyed. God will not lose one of His children.

Exodus 14:28-29 And the waters returned, and covered the chariots, and the horsemen, and all the host of Pharaoh that came into the sea after them; there remained not so much as one of them. But the children of Israel walked upon dry land in the midst of the sea; and the waters were a wall unto them on their right hand, and on their left.

God divided water from water when He delivered the children of Israel from bondage in Egypt.

When the children of Israel were delivered into the Promised Land it was accomplished by dividing waters from waters. This time it was the waters of the Jordan River.

Joshua 3:16 That the waters which came down from above stood and rose up upon an heap very far from the city Adam, that is beside Zaretan: and those that came down toward the sea of the plain, even the salt sea, failed, and were cut off: and the people passed over right against Jericho.

The "waters which came down from above", or the spirit, "stood and rose up". Those "that came down toward the sea", or the flesh, "failed and were cut off".

Water was often separated from water in the Bible; and water, blood or oil was often sprinkled in ceremonies. To sprinkle a liquid is to separate it into smaller pieces. Sprinkling a liquid does not divide it into two pieces as in the separation of flesh and spirit. A liquid is divided into many pieces by sprinkling, but it is the nations that are sprinkled. All the occasions in the Torah where blood, water or oil is sprinkled, it is symbolic of the Day of Judgment when the nations of Earth will be sprinkled.

Isaiah 52:15 So shall he sprinkle many nations; the kings shall shut their mouths at him: for that which had not been told them shall they see; and that which they had not heard shall they consider.

This description of what happens on the Day of Judgment is repeated in the New Testament. Instead of being sprinkled, in the New Testament the nations are said to be separated.

Matthew 25:32 And before him shall be gathered all nations: and he shall separate them one from another, as a shepherd divideth his sheep from the goats:

Many nations are separated, but they are divided into two groups, the sheep, and the goats. All the sprinkling in the Old Testament represents a separation into two groups.

The Biblical references to redemption by separation are abundant. There is the sprinkling of blood, the tearing of the veil, and the separation of waters from waters. This is just the beginning.

When gold is refined, the gold is separated from other metals or impurities.

Zechariah 13:9 And I will bring the third part through the fire, and will refine them as silver is refined, and will try them as gold is tried: they shall call on my name, and I will hear them: I will say, It is my people: and they shall say, The Lord is my God.

Yet another way in which the Bible reveals the plan of salvation is circumcision. Circumcision is when part of a person is removed.

When Elijah went up by a whirlwind to heaven, symbolic of the resurrection, Elisha tore his clothes in half.

2 Kings 2:12 And Elisha saw it, and he cried, My father, my father, the chariot of Israel, and the horsemen thereof. And he saw him no more: and he took hold of his own clothes, and rent them in two pieces.

Grace is the separation of the spirit from the flesh. Water which cleans things is often used in the Bible to symbolize or represent grace. The most important animal sacrifice was the sacrifice of a spotless heifer. The ashes of this sacrifice were referred to as a water of separation.

Numbers 19:9 And a man that is clean shall gather up the ashes of the heifer, and lay them up without the camp in a clean place, and it shall be kept for the congregation of the children of Israel for a water of separation: it is a purification for sin.

The ashes of the heifer were necessary to cleanse anyone who had touched a dead body or had been in the same building with a dead body. In Judaism a person must separate themselves from dead flesh.

We must be separated from (dead) flesh. Contact with dead flesh requires the water of separation.

Another indication of Grace by separation was the "vow of separation". A person who took this vow was called a Nazarite.

Numbers 6:5-6 All the days of the vow of his separation there shall no razor come upon his head: until the days be fulfilled, in the which he separateth himself unto the LORD, he shall be holy, and shall let the locks of the hair of his head grow. All the days that he separateth himself unto the LORD he shall come at no dead body.

Numbers 6:18 And the Nazarite shall shave the head of his separation at the door of the tabernacle of the congregation, and shall take the hair of the head of his separation, and put it in the fire which is under the sacrifice of the peace offerings.

A Nazarite is a representation of the spirit inside the child of God. A Nazarite must separate himself from dead flesh. They do not go near a dead body. The hair on the head of the Nazarite is shaved and burned in the fire. Just as the flesh is thrown in the fire after it is separated from the spirit.

In Matthew, chapter 24, the disciples asked Jesus about different events. He was asked about the destruction of the temple, and about His return.

Matthew 24:2-3 And Jesus said unto them, See ye not all these things? verily I say unto you, There shall not be left here one stone upon another, that shall not be thrown down. And as he sat upon the mount of Olives, the disciples came unto him privately, saying, Tell us, when shall these things be? and what shall be the sign of thy coming, and of the end of the world?

In His reply Jesus gave some details that could be referring to the destruction of the temple. He also gave some details that clearly seem to be pointing to His return, or the signs before His return. Jesus then seems to say that everything including His return will occur in the first century.

Matthew 24:34 Verily I say unto you, This generation shall not pass, till all these things be fulfilled.

Jesus did not say that everything would happen in the first century. What He said was this generation shall not pass, but Jesus is still alive. That generation has not passed yet.

This implies that the generation alive at that time would someday pass, but it will occur after the return of Christ. At some point after the return of Christ, Jesus will discard His flesh. It could be said at that time that the generation alive at the time of Christ has finally passed.

Revelation 3:12 Him that overcometh will I make a pillar in the temple of my God, and he shall go no more out: and I will write upon him the name of my God, and the name of the city of my God, which is new Jerusalem, which cometh down out of heaven from my God: and I will write upon him my new name.

At the end of creation Christ will have a new name. In the Bible, a new name marks a change in the person whose name is being changed like when Abram became Abraham or when Saul became Paul.

Christ is to have a new name, so there will be some kind of transition at the end of creation. At the end of creation Christ discards His fleshly body. What is fair for Christ is fair for everybody else. For when Christ receives a new name all the children of God will be called by another name.

Isaiah 65:15 And ye shall leave your name for a curse unto my chosen: for the Lord GOD shall slay thee, and call his servants by another name:

For Christ to discard His flesh and return to God does not mean that Christ will leave us. Christ returns to God at the end of the current timeline, but that only means that Christ is one with God outside of time. Christ prepares a place for us. This place may be another timeline, another universe, or another big bang. Christ will be with us in the place He prepares for us. Christ is God with us.

Whether it be circumcision, the Passover, or Nazarites, whether it be separating water from water or the sprinkling of blood, purification by separation is a dominant theme throughout the Old Testament. All this purification by separation is taken to mean separating good people from bad people.

Sometimes it is taken to mean separating us from our sin while retaining our flesh. Yet no sacrifice by someone else relieves us of our responsibility for sin so that our flesh deserves eternal life. The flesh is guilty and not worthy to enter the kingdom of God.

1 Corinthians 15:50 Now this I say, brethren, that flesh and blood cannot inherit the kingdom of God; neither doth corruption inherit incorruption.

Galatians 5:19-23 Now the works of the flesh are manifest, which are these; Adultery, fornication, uncleanness, lasciviousness, Idolatry, witchcraft, hatred, variance, emulations, wrath, strife, seditions, heresies, Envyings, murders, drunkenness, revellings, and such like: of the which I tell you before, as I have also told you in time past, that they which do such things shall not inherit the kingdom of God. But the fruit of the Spirit is love, joy, peace, longsuffering, gentleness, goodness, faith, Meekness, temperance: against such there is no law.

Paul talks about the "redemption of our body"; but he is talking about those who are the children of God. Those who have, "the firstfruits of the Spirit". Paul is talking about the child of God, but he is not referring to the entire child of God. He is only referring to those who "groan within ourselves".

Romans 8:23 And not only they, but ourselves also, which have the firstfruits of the Spirit, even we ourselves groan within ourselves, waiting for the adoption, to wit, the redemption of our body.

Paul is talking about the spirit "within" the child of God. The "we" who are redeemed are those who "groan within". "The redemption of our body" is referring to the spiritual body that is within the child of God. There is a natural body, and there is a spiritual body.

The apostle Paul often wrote of the spirit and the flesh. His words seemed to indicate that those who follow the Spirit are the children of God. Those who follow the flesh are bound for destruction. This is true but Paul is not always referring to two different groups of people. Often, he is referring to the two different people in each child of God. Paul often talks of the spirit and the flesh that make up one person as if they are two different people because with the grace of Christ, they are two different people.

Romans 8:1 There is therefore now no condemnation to them which are in Christ Jesus, who walk not after the flesh, but after the Spirit.

It is not true that Christians always walk after the Spirit while atheists always walk after the flesh. Christians will sin and walk after the flesh. Atheists can have compassion for others. This means they have a spirit and when they act on that spirit they are walking after the Spirit. It is the spirit itself within the child of God that always walks after the Spirit. The spirit within an atheist will walk after the Spirit.

The spirit within us cannot sin for it is love whether it be in a Christian or in an atheist. Likewise, in both groups, the flesh always walks after the flesh and is not capable of true righteousness.

To understand the writings of Paul, understand that good versus evil is not one group of people versus another group of people. It is not us against them. Paul talks of spirit against flesh not Christian against heathen. There is good and evil within all the children of God in all nations and religions. This good versus evil is the flesh against the spirit. This is the good and evil that is separated on the Day of Judgment.

To understand the writings of Paul always try to determine if he is talking about two different people or if he is talking about the spirit and flesh, the two different bodies in each child of God.

Romans 8:5-6 For they that are after the flesh do mind the things of the flesh; but they that are after the Spirit the things of the Spirit. For to be carnally minded is death; but to be spiritually minded is life and peace.

In this passage Paul is not talking about two different groups of people. "They that are after the flesh" and "they that are after the Spirit" are the same people. Each child of God contains both a natural mind and a spiritual mind. For the carnal mind is death but for the spiritual mind is life. Paul said that he sometimes followed the flesh.

Romans 7:17-24 Now then it is no more I that do it, but sin that dwelleth in me. For I know that in me (that is, in my flesh,) dwelleth no good thing: for to will is present with me; but how to perform that which is good I find not. For the good that I would I do not: but the evil which I would not, that I do. Now if I do that I would not, it is no more I that do it, but sin that dwelleth in me. I find then a law, that, when I would do good, evil is present with me. For I delight in the law of God after the inward man: But I see another law in my members, warring against the law of my mind, and bringing me into captivity to the law of sin which is in my members. O wretched man that I am! who shall deliver me from the body of this death?

If we feel love, if we perform charity, if we do any good thing, it comes from our spiritual body. If we behave selfishly it comes from our natural body. The natural man, which is our physical body, is not capable of righteousness.

Romans 8:8 So then they that are in the flesh cannot please God.

1 Corinthians 2:14 But the natural man receiveth not the things of the Spirit of God: for they are foolishness unto him: neither can he know them, because they are spiritually discerned.

We are currently both spirit and flesh, and we follow both the Spirit and the flesh. Sometimes we are good and compassionate and sometimes we are selfish or self-righteous. Within each of us, the spirit always follows the Spirit, and the flesh always follows the flesh.

Romans 8:3-4 For what the law could not do, in that it was weak through the flesh, God sending his own Son in the likeness of sinful flesh, and for sin, condemned sin in the flesh: That the righteousness of the law might be fulfilled in us, who walk not after the flesh, but after the Spirit.

Paul said the law was weak through the flesh meaning the Law could not provide righteousness. Satan manipulated the flesh to destroy the children of God including the spirits inside the children of God. Satan made the Law unrighteous in that the spirits of love would have to be destroyed under the Law. Christ fulfilled "the righteousness of the law" by making the Law just. Thanks to Christ, the Law does not destroy the spirit. With the Grace of Christ, the spirit is judged separately from the flesh.

The spirit in the child of God comes from God. The spirit is love and all love comes from God. The spirit walks after the Spirit and is bound for life. The flesh walks after the flesh and is bound for death. If we commit both sin and righteousness, if we possess both flesh and spirit then we are bound for both death and life. We must each become two people for this to be possible.

Romans 8:10 And if Christ be in you, the body is dead because of sin; but the Spirit is life because of righteousness.

Even those who have lived and died without ever hearing the name "Jesus", even those who do not believe in God will live again in the kingdom of Heaven if the Love of God is in their heart. Because of Christ all the children of God in all nations and religions will fairly deserve eternal life.

Christ is God but being a Spirit born into flesh, He is also fully human. Since Christ discards His flesh, it becomes completely fair for our flesh to be discarded. Our soul along with the spirit of love within us is judged as a separate person. This idea may seem simplistic, but it reconciles supposed contradictions in the Bible. It is also confirmed by having been unnoticed by billions of people despite its remarkable simplicity and the great abundance of separation in the Bible.

Granted, there may have been millions of times when a Christian considered the idea of God separating the spirit from the flesh, but God could easily cause it to be quickly forgotten every single time. Only Divine intervention can explain how the simple ideas contained in this book could have been kept secret.

None of our sin comes from our spirit. Our spirit is not merely forgiven; the spirit of love within us is perfect. On the Day of Judgment our spirit is found worthy of eternal life and is given a new body. This is the "grace" of Christ. This is how the Messiah redeems the children of God. It means that all good people are given eternal life in Heaven by Christ.

Chapter 7 – The Two Objectives of Judgment

To reconcile the Bible, and make many riddles disappear, it must be understood that the words salvation, saved, heaven, and hell can all be used to refer to eternal judgment, but they can also be used by the Bible to refer to temporal judgment on this side of eternity.

Jesus said that He is the only way to the Father. This is clearly referring to eternal Heaven, but this statement does not tell us what we must do to enter eternal Heaven. In other passages we are told we must do one thing or another, but these passages are not necessarily talking about eternal Heaven. Jesus clearly used the words kingdom of God to describe a heaven or a reward in this life.

Luke 17:20-21 And when he was demanded of the Pharisees, when the kingdom of God should come, he answered them and said, The kingdom of God cometh not with observation: Neither shall they say, Lo here! or, lo there! for, behold, the kingdom of God is within you.

God allows evil to exist, confined within time, to achieve the purpose of creation. The time is coming when God will destroy all evil, and that is the Day of Judgment. There will be no sin or imperfection entering the kingdom of God. Since we are part evil, we must be destroyed on the Day of Judgment. Fortunately, Christ redeems us by justifying the discarding of our flesh as explained in chapter five. This leaves us worthy of eternal life in the kingdom of God.

This is entirely a gift of God through Christ. Nothing we can do, including becoming a Christian or "accepting" Jesus provides us with this redemption. We must be perfect to be given eternal life on the Day of Judgment. Fortunately for us, the grace of Christ causes all children of God to be perfect.

Temporal judgment or judgment in time has a completely different objective from the Day of Judgment. It is a measured judgment that takes place before the Day of Judgment. Temporal judgment is about handing out measured punishment for sin and measured reward for righteousness. God executes perfect justice before the Day of Judgment.

When the Law was given to Moses, it was not understood to be referring to eternal life. It was believed to be referring to punishment or reward in this world.

Exodus 14:13 And Moses said unto the people, Fear ye not, stand still, and see the salvation of the Lord, which he will shew to you to day: for the Egyptians whom ye have seen to day, ye shall see them again no more for ever.

The Torah uses the word "salvation" to refer to God's deliverance and blessings on Earth. Some provisions of the Law of Moses appear to be pointing to the Day of Judgment like the death sentence for numerous offenses, but there was no concept of resurrection and eternal life at that time. Only recently before Christ did belief in resurrection and eternal judgment emerge in Judaism. The Law and judgment in the Jewish Scriptures were believed to be in this life. God would punish, or reward Israel based on their observance of the Law.

John 9:2 And his disciples asked him, saying, Master, who did sin, this man, or his parents, that he was born blind?

People at the time of Christ commonly believed that suffering in this life was punishment for sin. Punishment and salvation were both believed to refer to this world. Christ explained that suffering is not necessarily a result of sin.

Luke 13:1-5 There were present at that season some that told him of the Galilaeans, whose blood Pilate had mingled with their sacrifices. And

Jesus answering said unto them, Suppose ye that these Galilaeans were sinners above all the Galilaeans, because they suffered such things? I tell you, Nay: but, except ye repent, ye shall all likewise perish. Or those eighteen, upon whom the tower in Siloam fell, and slew them, think ye that they were sinners above all men that dwelt in Jerusalem? I tell you, Nay: but, except ye repent, ye shall all likewise perish.

Some people were killed by Pilate, and others were killed by a collapsed tower. These events had nothing to do with eternal Heaven; they were tragedies that occurred in this world. One tragedy was caused by human evil, and the other was caused by natural forces. Neither tragedy was caused by the sins of the victims.

Christ did not deny that there is punishment in this life for sin. He said that we should not look at those who suffer as being responsible for their suffering. Suffering is caused by natural forces, like cancer or an earthquake or a collapsed tower. Suffering can also be caused by human evil, like war or crime or those killed by Pilate.

Temporal judgment means our suffering will equal our sin, and our reward will equal our righteousness. Temporal judgment is less likely to be about cancer or earthquakes. It is more likely about our being able to deal with whatever comes. It is arrogant to look at someone who is suffering and seeing them as a sinner because they are suffering. Perhaps their suffering is greater than their sins and God will repay them. There is a good chance that their sins are less than the sins of those who judge them.

Physical suffering is mostly caused by evil or natural forces, not as punishment by God. Temporal judgment means that God will balance the scales in some manner before the Day of Judgment. Balancing the scales may mean that God helps someone through a difficult time, so they did not suffer as much as they appeared to suffer.

Numbers 14:18 The LORD is longsuffering, and of great mercy, forgiving iniquity and transgression, and by no means clearing the guilty, visiting the iniquity of the fathers upon the children unto the third and fourth generation.

The iniquity of one generation is visited on another. Visiting does not mean that the next generation is punished for the sins of the previous generation. The iniquity of one generation can impact the lives of their children and grandchildren. A wicked generation might cause an economic collapse and the next generation also experiences poverty. If the next generation is righteous, they may have great joy in their poverty. In this way, temporal judgment is less likely to be about wealth or poverty. It is less likely to be the cause of earthquakes or cancer. It is more likely to be spiritual.

Repentance does not save us on the Day of Judgment, Jesus saves us on the Day of Judgment. Repentance can sometimes save us from suffering in this life, whether it be caused by natural or evil forces.

Being saved from natural forces like cancer does not necessarily mean being cured of the cancer. It can mean God helps us endure whatever we are going through. Another reason we should not judge those who are suffering is we cannot know how much they are suffering. A person dying of cancer may be experiencing a close relationship with God.

We are saved on the Day of Judgment entirely by Christ. On the Day of Judgment, the Lord redeems His children, yet we still sin and are subject to temporal punishment. When the Bible talks about heaven, hell, redemption, salvation, or being saved, it is often talking about temporal judgment.

Any passage in the Bible in which punishment or reward is measured is referring to temporal judgment. Christ saves us on the Day of Judgment, anything else that saves us, must be saving us from temporal judgment. If we look at the following debate between the early Christians, they seem to believe that they were debating what is necessary to enter eternal Heaven.

Acts 15:1-2 And certain men which came down from Judaea taught the brethren, and said, Except ye be circumcised after the manner of Moses, ye cannot be saved. When therefore Paul and Barnabas had no small dissension and disputation with them, they determined that Paul and Barnabas, and certain other of them, should go up to Jerusalem unto the apostles and elders about this question.

Acts 15:5 But there rose up certain of the sect of the Pharisees which believed, saying, That it was needful to circumcise them, and to command them to keep the law of Moses.

Perhaps they did believe that our decisions and actions in this life can determine our eternal destiny. This is a universal assumption in Christianity. As it turns out, this belief was not clearly recorded in any of the books or letters that have been determined to be inspired by God and assembled into the book called the Bible.

God may have used men who believed we must be a Christian to get to Heaven. He used them to record a message which in its entirety communicates that God will redeem all His children. God will redeem His children who never heard of Jesus. The debate in this passage is concluded with Peter expressing the belief we shall be saved by grace.

Acts 15:11 But we believe that through the grace of the Lord Jesus Christ we shall be saved, even as they.

We are saved to eternal Heaven by Christ, yet by our words and actions we can be saved in temporal judgment. With early Judaism every reference to judgment was believed to be temporal judgment in this life. With Christianity that was transformed into a belief that all references to judgment are referring to eternal Heaven. Christians will sometimes mention temporal judgment, but they tend to believe that all Biblical references to heaven, salvation and being saved are referring to eternal life on the Day of Judgment. Even in the New Testament we see that this is not true.

In the book of Acts new converts to the faith were said to be saved.

> *Acts 2:47 Praising God, and having favour with all the people. And the Lord added to the church daily such as should be saved.*

A few verses earlier, in encouraging people to join the church, Peter stated what they were being saved from.

> *Acts 2:40 And with many other words did he testify and exhort, saying, Save yourselves from this untoward generation.*

A blind man called out for Jesus to heal him. He had faith that Jesus could heal him, and because of his faith, Jesus did heal him.

> *Luke 18:42-43 And Jesus said unto him, Receive thy sight: thy faith hath saved thee. And immediately he received his sight, and followed him, glorifying God: and all the people, when they saw it, gave praise unto God.*

His faith saved him, but he was not saved unto eternal life, he was saved from a life of blindness.

> *Matthew 28:18-20 And Jesus came and spake unto them, saying, All power is given unto me in heaven and in earth. Go ye therefore, and teach all nations, baptizing them in the name of the Father, and of the Son, and of the Holy Ghost: Teaching them to observe all things whatsoever I have commanded you: and, lo, I am with you always, even unto the end of the world. Amen.*

This is called the "great commission". The great commission is universally understood to be the command of Christ for Christians to go throughout the world and convert people to Christianity. Many Christians have dedicated their life to this cause. It has been done with a belief that there are eternal consequences for accepting or rejecting the gospel of Christ.

The great commission is not talking about eternal salvation. Jesus has already provided all His children with eternal life on the Day of Judgment. The great commission is about temporal judgment. It is about promoting righteousness in this life so people can have more joy and less suffering in this life.

Christians tend to believe that punishment for sin and reward for righteousness must be eternal, otherwise there is no reason for a person to avoid sin or try to be righteous. Just because temporal punishment for sin is not eternal does not mean it is trivial. A murder can cause the friends and family of the victim to experience grief and heartache for many years. The murderer should not be given leniency when he has the good fortune for that not to be the case.

The murderer may be a child of God who is loved by God. He may be given eternal life in Heaven by the grace of Christ. Since God also loves the murder victim and all who mourn their death, the murderer will pay an enormous price. The murderer must pay an enormous price for the suffering that he caused. The fair punishment for our sins can be much harsher than we realize.

> *Matthew 5:22 But I say unto you, That whosoever is angry with his brother without a cause shall be in danger of the judgment: and whosoever shall say to his brother, Raca, shall be in danger of the council: but whosoever shall say, Thou fool, shall be in danger of hell fire.*

We will suffer greatly if we intentionally hurt someone's feelings with rudeness and insults. Such insults can cause a lot of pain. How much more when we commit great offenses that can cause others much suffering. We will even regret our tendency to go through our day with a callous disregard for others.

Punishment for sin can be much harsher than we realize. Reward for righteousness can be much greater than we realize even though it is not eternal. Punishment for sin is an eye for an eye, but Jesus implied that the reward for righteousness will be multiplied by up to one hundred.

Mark 10:30 But he shall receive an hundredfold now in this time, houses, and brethren, and sisters, and mothers, and children, and lands, with persecutions; and in the world to come eternal life.

When we are righteous, God may reward us with far greater joy than the joy we give to others. It is believed that those who lived righteous lives are already in Heaven, but this would be very few people.

Matthew 7:14 Because strait is the gate, and narrow is the way, which leadeth unto life, and few there be that find it.

Thanks to Christ, many people will make it to Heaven on the Day of Judgment, but this passage is talking about temporal judgment as it something we find or earn. There are only a few people who are given a Heavenly reward before the Day of Judgment. This is why Catholics pray to the saints. It is believed that the saints are already in Heaven. A person who devotes their life to loving God and helping others will be rewarded immensely before the Day of Judgment. The saints may be given centuries in Heaven before the Day of Judgment. After the Day of Judgment, all the children of God will be equal in the kingdom of God.

Matthew 20:1-5 For the kingdom of heaven is like unto a man that is an householder, which went out early in the morning to hire labourers into his vineyard. And when he had agreed with the labourers for a penny a day, he sent them into his vineyard. And he went out about the third hour, and saw others standing idle in the marketplace, And said unto them; Go ye also into the vineyard, and whatsoever is right I will give you. And they went their way. Again he went out about the sixth and ninth hour, and did likewise.

Matthew 20:8-9 So when even was come, the lord of the vineyard saith unto his steward, Call the labourers, and give them their hire, beginning from the last unto the first. And when they came that were hired about the eleventh hour, they received every man a penny.

In this parable, some laborers worked more hours and gathered more fruit than others. This is temporal judgment where there is measured reward for righteousness. The fruit was gathered during the workday, and it represents the reward for our righteousness during our lifetime even if that reward may come after death but before the Day of Judgment.

The workers all receive the same amount of pay at the end of the workday. This represents eternal Heaven after the Day of Judgment. The murderer and the saint will have the same reward in eternal Heaven. The saint will be greatly rewarded before the Day of Judgment, and the murderer will be extremely punished before the Day of Judgment.

The justice of God is "an eye for an eye", but it does not result in two blind men. Only the person who commits the offense is punished. The justice of God is measured out against everyone individually. If you harm your enemy, that harm may be counted as punishment for the person you harmed. God will reduce in equal measure some other punishment that they would have otherwise received.

If you cause someone to suffer unjustly, then God will repay them.

You can impact how they are punished, but you cannot add to the suffering of your enemy, unless you cause your enemy to retaliate so they increase their sins. Otherwise, when you harm your enemy,

motivated by hatred, you can only add to your own sin and your own punishment.

Deuteronomy 32:35 To me belongeth vengeance and recompence; their foot shall slide in due time: for the day of their calamity is at hand, and the things that shall come upon them make haste.

This is what is meant by vengeance is mine saith the Lord. No one will add to the suffering of anyone else. We can only add to our own suffering.

When the Bible says we must do one thing or another to go to Heaven, it may be talking about eternal Heaven determined on the Day of Judgment. Whatever it says is required of us to enter eternal Heaven, our spirit has met that requirement. Our spirit is found worthy of eternal life even if we have clearly failed to meet that requirement. A sinner can have a sinless spirit within themselves. It is that sinless spirit that is worthy of eternal life in Heaven on the Day of Judgment.

The spirit within us is the true child of God. An atheist can have a spirit within themselves that is sinless and believes in the "name" or essence of God. Our spirit meets the requirements of God thanks to the grace of Christ separating our spirit from our flesh.

Matthew 19:29 And every one that hath forsaken houses, or brethren, or sisters, or father, or mother, or wife, or children, or lands, for my name's sake, shall receive an hundredfold, and shall inherit everlasting life.

In this verse there is a measured reward for righteousness. The Day of Judgment is not a measured reward, and this is therefore temporal judgment. A hundredfold reward does suggest that the reward for righteousness can be immense. There is also an unearned inheritance of eternal life on the Day of Judgment. The hundredfold reward and the inheritance are presented as two different things, because they are two different things. They are two different objectives of judgment.

The children of God who lose the hundredfold reward due to their sinfulness will still get the unearned inheritance of eternal life. A hundredfold is a multiplication of a value, so there must be a value to be multiplied. There must be an act of righteousness to be rewarded. Inheritances tend to be unearned.

Matthew 7:21 Not every one that saith unto me, Lord, Lord, shall enter into the kingdom of heaven; but he that doeth the will of my Father which is in heaven.

This is talking about eternal Heaven, but it is only the spirit within us which does the will of God. Even people who never heard of Jesus can have a spirit within themselves that does the will of God.

Acts 4:12 Neither is there salvation in any other: for there is none other name under heaven given among men, whereby we must be saved.

This is clearly eternal salvation, as it is salvation that is only by Christ. This verse does not call on us to do anything, even to be a Christian. We are saved by Christ and not by anything we have done or will do.

Romans 5:8-10 But God commendeth his love toward us, in that, while we were yet sinners, Christ died for us. Much more then, being now justified by his blood, we shall be saved from wrath through him. For if, when we were enemies, we were reconciled to God by the death of his Son, much more, being reconciled, we shall be saved by his life.

We were in a fallen state when Christ died for us, but we are now justified. We are now redeemed to eternal life. How much shall we be saved from wrath (in this life). This verse does not actually say that we must be Christian to be justified. Paul is speaking to the church in Rome, but he does not deny that other people can be justified.

Christians disagree on the question of eternal security. They believe our redemption to eternal life in Heaven is achieved by our words and actions in this life. Often, they believe that the act that saves us to eternal life is finding or accepting Jesus as our Savior. But if we find Jesus, can we lose Him?

If our eternal destiny is based on what we do, then we can change our eternal destiny if we change what we do. If a Christian were to leave the church and return to sin, they may lose their redemption.

We can backslide into sin and completely reject God, yet we are told that the children of God cannot lose their redemption.

John 10:27-29 My sheep hear my voice, and I know them, and they follow me: And I give unto them eternal life; and they shall never perish, neither shall any man pluck them out of my hand. My Father, which gave them me, is greater than all; and no man is able to pluck them out of my Father's hand.

John 5:24 Verily, verily, I say unto you, He that heareth my word, and believeth on him that sent me, hath everlasting life, and shall not come into condemnation; but is passed from death unto life.

Our redemption is entirely because of Christ. It is only our spirit that is redeemed. That redemption cannot be lost as our spirit is worthy of eternal life. If we follow our flesh, if we leave the church and return to sin, we will suffer for it. But it is suffering in temporal hell, not eternal hell. We will miss out on temporal heaven, not eternal Heaven. We will still be redeemed to eternal life on the Day of Judgment.

This is why the Bible can both support and reject the security of our salvation. We have eternal security for eternal life on the Day of Judgment. We can backslide into sin and suffer temporal judgment.

Our flesh commits sin, but our spirit follows the Law.

Matthew 22:37-40 Jesus said unto him, Thou shalt love the Lord thy God with all thy heart, and with all thy soul, and with all thy mind. This is the first and great commandment. And the second is like unto it, Thou shalt love thy neighbour as thyself. On these two commandments hang all the law and the prophets.

Christ only had two commandments, to love God and to love our neighbor. The two commandments are the basis for all the law and the prophets. This is the Law by which we are judged. There were other rules that existed for other purposes.

In the Bible, the punishment for homosexuality was death, but this does not mean that homosexuals will be killed on the Day of Judgment. Homosexuality undermines marriage which is an essential institution for society to thrive. The whole point of creation is marriage and children and the journey of life. God is not against people who are homosexual. God loves all His children.

Homosexuality is not intrinsically greater a sin than heterosexuality. It is a mechanical act. All sex can be sinful depending on our feelings for ourselves and the other person. The rules about homosexuality are for the benefit of society. They are not because God is against people who are gay.

This does not mean that the rule against homosexuality is trivial. For society to survive, young adults need to have children. People grow old and die. They must be replaced. Family and children are the whole point of creation.

Matthew 5:28 But I say unto you, That whosoever looketh on a woman to lust after her hath committed adultery with her already in his heart.

Any lust, heterosexual or not, that is not acted upon still makes us unworthy of eternal life. It is part of our fallen nature of selfishness that makes us unworthy to enter the perfect kingdom of God. We will not be punished in this life in temporal judgment for lust or hostility that we are able to overcome.

Judaism rejects the idea that thoughts that are not acted upon can be a sin, but in Judaism judgment is focused on the here and now. Judaism is correct; we are not punished in the here and now for thoughts we are able to overcome. Christianity is focused entirely on the world to come. Christianity is also correct; we are not worthy to enter the perfect kingdom of God because of our hatred and lust, even if we do not act upon it.

There is judgment in the here and now, and there is judgment in the world to come. We are not punished in the here and now for our sinful thoughts that we do not act upon, but they do leave us unworthy to enter the perfect Kingdom of God.

The Jews were expecting the Messiah to establish the kingdom in the here and now. Jesus established the kingdom of God in the hereafter. Perfection, including no hostility or lust, is required to enter the eternal kingdom that Christ established when He died on the cross. When He died on the cross, Jesus made it possible for us to be perfect, and worthy to enter the kingdom He established.

Jesus was asked what we must do to have eternal life (in Heaven).

Mark 10:17 And when he was gone forth into the way, there came one running, and kneeled to him, and asked him, Good Master, what shall I do that I may inherit eternal life?

Jesus tells the man to give away all he has.

Mark 10:21 Then Jesus beholding him loved him, and said unto him, One thing thou lackest: go thy way, sell whatsoever thou hast, and give to the poor, and thou shalt have treasure in heaven: and come, take up the cross, and follow me.

If you look at the response of Jesus in its entirety, we must be perfect to have eternal life. Jesus points out that it is impossible for us to be perfect, but with God all things are possible. God can even cause humans to be perfect.

Mark 10:25-27 It is easier for a camel to go through the eye of a needle, than for a rich man to enter into the kingdom of God. And they were astonished out of measure, saying among themselves, Who then can be saved? And Jesus looking upon them saith, With men it is impossible, but not with God: for with God all things are possible.

We must be perfect to enter the kingdom of God, and we cannot be perfect unless God makes us perfect. Giving away our possessions will not make us perfect, and it is not necessarily essential for us to achieve perfection. If you work and build something, it is not required that you give it away. Jesus told him to give away his possessions because he will not need them. He must be perfect to earn eternal life. If he is perfect, God will take of him, and he will want for nothing.

While we cannot achieve perfection, God can cause us to be perfect. We are made perfect by discarding our flesh. This is how God can cause us to be perfect in a way that does not contradict the Scriptures. The spirit within us, the true child of God, does not commit sins.

The idea that we must be perfect is common in the Bible. The Bible also supports the idea that the children of God are perfect.

Matthew 5:48 Be ye therefore perfect, even as your Father which is in heaven is perfect.

We must be perfect. On the Day of Judgment everything we have said and done will be judged.

Matthew 12:36 But I say unto you, That every idle word that men shall speak, they shall give account thereof in the day of judgment.

Revelation 20:12 And I saw the dead, small and great, stand before God; and the books were opened: and another book was opened, which is the book of life: and the dead were judged out of those things which were written in the books, according to their works.

This seems to set an impossible standard. We are told that flesh cannot enter heaven.

1 Corinthians 15:50 Now this I say, brethren, that flesh and blood cannot inherit the kingdom of God; neither doth corruption inherit incorruption.

But the seed or the spirit within us is perfect.

1 John 3:9 Whosoever is born of God doth not commit sin; for his seed remaineth in him: and he cannot sin, because he is born of God.

Christians do not take this verse literally. They would say that we are not perfect, but our sins are washed away causing us to be sinless. If we take this verse literally, we have no sins to wash away. We can take this verse literally because the spirit within us is the true child of God that does not sin. We have sins while in the flesh, but our flesh will be washed away.

John 6:44 No man can come to me, except the Father which hath sent me draw him: and I will raise him up at the last day.

John 15:16 Ye have not chosen me, but I have chosen you, and ordained you, that ye should go and bring forth fruit, and that your fruit should remain: that whatsoever ye shall ask of the Father in my name, he may give it you.

Romans 8:28-30 And we know that all things work together for good to them that love God, to them who are the called according to his purpose. For whom he did foreknow, he also did predestinate to be conformed to

the image of his Son, that he might be the firstborn among many
brethren. Moreover whom he did predestinate, them he also called: and
whom he called, them he also justified: and whom he justified, them he
also glorified.

The perfect spirit of love within us came from God, and God predetermined who would be born with the spirit. Even predestination can be taken literally. It does not conflict with our being judged based on our works. It is also true that we only make it to Heaven through Christ.

Luke 14:12-14 Then said he also to him that bade him, When thou
makest a dinner or a supper, call not thy friends, nor thy brethren, neither
thy kinsmen, nor thy rich neighbours; lest they also bid thee again, and a
recompence be made thee. But when thou makest a feast, call the poor, the
maimed, the lame, the blind: And thou shalt be blessed; for they cannot
recompense thee: for thou shalt be recompensed at the resurrection of the
just.

This passage seems to say there is a reward at the resurrection for our actions in this life. Eternal life at the resurrection is entirely a gift of Christ. This verse is not talking about a reward in eternal Heaven because Jesus specifies the resurrection of the just. The resurrection of the just would be the first resurrection. The first resurrection is for the millennium or the Messianic Age which is the fulfillment of the sabbath.

Revelation 20:6 Blessed and holy is he that hath part in the first
resurrection: on such the second death hath no power, but they shall be
priests of God and of Christ, and shall reign with him a thousand years.

In the eternal kingdom of God, we will love each other equally. Heaven will not be divided into families where we love some people more than others because they are in our family. In Heaven our earthly relationships will be forgotten, and we will love each other equally. God knows we want to reunite with our loved ones. This is why Jesus said that the sabbath was made for man, and not man for the sabbath.

Revelation 20:2-3 And he laid hold on the dragon, that old serpent, which is the Devil, and Satan, and bound him a thousand years, And cast him into the bottomless pit, and shut him up, and set a seal upon him, that he should deceive the nations no more, till the thousand years should be fulfilled: and after that he must be loosed a little season.

The sabbath is the Messianic Age where God gives us a thousand years on the Earth to be with our family and friends, but this is only for the children of God. Only the children of God are resurrected at the first resurrection. That is what is meant by the resurrection of the just. The second death is said to have no power over those resurrected at the first resurrection. The second death is the Day of Judgement. Everyone will be resurrected after the Messianic Age for the Day of Judgment. The millennium is before the Day of Judgment, so there can still be reward for righteousness during the millennium.

The Messianic Age will be a return to the Garden of Eden. It will be the first one thousand years of Heaven. It will be on the Earth, and we will have the memories of our lifetime. There will be no suffering, death, or birth. The devil will be bound, and there will be no evil or sin.

The sabbath represents a thousand years of rest we will have to be with our family and friends before we enter the eternal kingdom of God.

Chapter 8 – The Promised Restoration of Israel

The Messiah is supposed to gather the Jewish people back to the land of Israel, but Israel has already been gathered and modern Israel has fulfilled prophecies without the appearance of the Messiah. Some rabbis say that prophecy is being fulfilled in a non-miraculous way because of certain modern conditions. This seems like a poor excuse. The Messiah leads the restoration of Israel. There must have been a Messiah when Israel was restored.

Even if the Lord is causing the events to occur, there must be a human Messiah leading the way.

Historically, religious Jews would often refuse to return to the land of Israel because they were waiting for the Messiah. Charles Darwin and growing secularism along with persecution caused secular Jews to restore Israel without a Messiah. Zionism led to the persecution of Jews in the Middle East, causing a flood of Jewish asylum seekers moving to Israel. The decline of the Ottoman Empire made it all possible, and it is miraculous how everything fell into place after almost two thousand years.

Regardless of how it happened, the restoration of a nation after two thousand years is miraculous. The survival of Israel in such a hostile region is also remarkable. Instead of making excuses for why the Messiah did not gather the Jews, we should consider the possibility that the Messiah did gather the Jews. If the Lord has been helping Israel, even leading Israel to miraculous military victories as in the Six-Day War, then perhaps the Lord is the Messiah.

This idea will not be given any consideration by non-religious Jews as they are not looking for the Messiah. For religious Jews, the idea that the Lord could be the Messiah is very problematic.

The Messiah is a human, and if he has already restored Israel, then he must have been born sometime in the past. If the Messiah is also the Lord, it means He must be a human who was born sometime in the past, who is also the Lord.

Christianity is nothing more than many different interpretations of the teachings of a first century Jewish rabbi, who claimed to be the Messiah, and who also claimed to be the Lord. Jewish scholars overwhelmingly rejected his claim since the Messiah is a man and a man cannot be the Lord. But what if the Lord wants to be a man for some reason? Is God able to create that condition?

There are clues in the Scriptures indicating that the Messiah would be Divine, but the idea of a Divine human seems impossible. With many centuries to anticipate the coming of Messiah, the Jews developed theories that had no resemblance to Jesus dying on a cross. It is only natural that the Jews rejected Jesus. The Gentiles had no preconceived notions about the Messiah, and they were able to see how Jesus fulfilled many Jewish prophecies in remarkable detail.

Considering that the Messiah does great things for us, the Messiah would have to be Divine. If the Messiah is our redeemer, He is doing something that God would do Himself. We will not spend eternity being grateful to a human. If the Messiah merely brings utopia in the world, it still seems odd that God would use a fully human Messiah. It seems odd that we would be so grateful to a human. The Scriptures portray the Messiah as someone with exalted significance, much greater than anyone who ever lived.

The Messiah defeats the enemies of God and establishes the Kingdom. This most significantly applies to the eternal Kingdom, not the kingdom of the Messiah on Earth that will come later. More important than an earthly kingdom, Jesus has already defeated the enemies of God and established the Kingdom of God in the world to come. The idea of resurrection to eternal life only appeared in Judaism not long before Christ. This was after the Jews had already developed theories of the coming Messiah. They were not looking for a Messiah to establish a Kingdom in the world to come.

Over time Christian theology interpreted the words of Christ in ways that contradicted the Jewish Scriptures. Jesus was not punished for our sins. It was over a thousand years after Christ when Christians came to commonly believe that Jesus was punished for our sins.

Jesus can be reconciled to Judaism.

Christians don't see a problem with their inconsistencies with Judaism, and Jews don't realize the significance of reconciling the most dominant figure in history with the religion He fulfilled.

Jewish scholars say there is nothing to indicate a Messiah who comes a second time, but Mosses went up the mountain to be with God, and then he came back down. This was not a second coming of Mosses, but only a return. If the Messiah is a human who is also the Lord, He can overcome death. He can have the longevity to be a two-thousand-year-old human. Still alive and intervening in human affairs to restore Israel. If Jesus is still alive; He may yet cause the temple to be rebuilt and fulfill all the other prophecies of the Messiah during his first, and only (very long) lifetime.

"Second coming" is misleading. There is one coming, one lifetime that is currently almost two thousand years long. If the Messiah is the Lord, all other objections to Jesus as the Messiah disappear.

Jesus is the Messiah of Israel Who will return to Israel.

The belief that the Jews are the chosen people of God does not mean that God is against other people. There is a remarkable story being told. The different nations and religions are like actors playing different roles. Some are good guys, and some are bad guys. God can have children in every nation and religion. We are judged as individuals, but the nations tell a story.

God told Abraham that through his seed the world would be blessed. The nation of Israel was born in bondage like the spirit born into the flesh. Moses led Israel out of bondage just as the spirit is separated from the flesh. Moses and numerous prophets foretold a coming Messiah.

Jesus was rejected and killed, rose from the dead, and ascended to Heaven. Jesus fulfilled many prophecies remarkably. A large part of the world came to see Jesus as the promised Jewish Messiah even though He has always been rejected by most Jews. Until now no one was able to reconcile His words with the Jewish Scriptures.

Shortly after Christ, Israel was scattered among the nations as foretold.

Then came Mohammed who claimed to be a prophet of the God of Israel. When the Jews rejected his claim, Mohammed became hostile to the Jews. Israel is now restored from the nations as foretold. Israel is surrounded by enemies as foretold. The enemies are the children of Ishmael. They are the followers of Mohammed who are determined to destroy Israel because the Jews rejected Mohammed.

This brings us to the current conflict in the Middle East.

All nations were built by force as all land has been conquered militarily, but the Jews moved to a remote province in a crumbling empire, a barren wasteland. They purchased the wasteland and transformed it into a prosperous society. The growing economy that the Jews built attracted people from the region looking for jobs. This meant the Arab population in Palestine was growing because of the growing Jewish population.

There had been a significant Jewish population in Palestine long before modern Zionism. Whether you call it Palestine, Israel or Judea, there has been a significant Jewish presence in that part of the world for thousands of years. With the end of the Ottoman Empire, the Jews would be one of the groups which would be given their own nation as this empire was broken apart.

This is only reasonable. Various groups that had been controlled by an empire should have been given their independence when that empire collapsed. Whether or not other groups were treated fairly does not affect the fairness of giving the Jews a homeland.

Just looking at the Jewish presence in the Muslim world in recent centuries, the land that went to Israel in 1948 was not overly generous. It was a tiny sliver of land. This tiny sliver of land was incredibly modest especially when compared to the property and wealth that the Jews lost in the Muslim world as they were expelled from many Muslim nations throughout much of the 20th century. Jews expelled from Muslim nations were welcomed as citizens in Israel. Muslims who voluntarily left Israel have descendants still living in refugee camps in Muslim lands.

Again, this is not basing Jewish claims to the land on the Bible or on Jewish ownership of the land two thousand years ago. Jewish land and wealth in the Muslim world that was seized by the Muslims was greater than the tiny sliver of land that went to Israel in 1948. This is especially true considering that the land that went to Israel had been mostly wasteland before it was transformed by the Jews.

The Jews also purchased the land from the rightful owners. They often overpaid for wasteland which they developed into a modern nation. The fact that they did not take the land by force but purchased it from the legal owners is somehow seen by many people as an act of aggression.

A corrupt and violent humanity believes purchasing the land somehow gives the Jews less claim to the land. All other nations were built by force, so Israel actually has a far greater claim to their land than any other nation. The Jews then won more land in multiple defensive wars against an enemy determined to commit genocide. This gives them an even greater claim to the land. The Jews have greater claim to their land, including Gaza and the West Bank, than any other nation.

In the Six Day War, the Israelis won Gaza and the West Bank and other territories from the Muslims. This was after several Muslim nations almost surrounded and promised to destroy Israel. Based on the rules that human nations have lived by throughout history, Gaza and the West Bank should go to Israel. The Muslims were the aggressor, but Israel was the victor. This means that according to the rules of human nations, the land belongs to Israel.

God not only gave the land of Israel to the Jews as stated in the Bible; God also arranged the conditions in modern times so that the land does rightfully belong to the Jews in every way. Yet in the current reality foreseen by God, most people of the world cannot see that Israel clearly owns this land. Most people cannot see the overwhelming claim that Israel has to the land because of the lies told by those who seek to destroy Israel.

It is claimed that all the non-Jews who lived in Israel in 1967 are a separate and distinct nationality called the Palestinians. This lie is central to all the efforts to demonize Israel.

The only difference between the Arabs of Palestine and other Arabs in the region is the pattern of clothing they wear. Before modern times there was never a Palestinian nation, or a Palestinian language, or a Palestinian culture. There was never a Palestinian nationalist movement of any kind.

They use the name Palestine, but the Arabs have no historical connection to the name Palestine. The name Palestine comes from the Romans. Even the ancient Philistines from whom the name Palestine was derived were from southern Europe and had no connection to the Arabs.

Before 1967 when Jordan controlled the West Bank, the Arabs of Palestine had no desire for their own nation. They used the name West Bank acknowledging that they lived in the west bank of Jordan. This is an acknowledgement that they did not want independence, at least not from Jordan.

It was in the early 1960s when the Palestinian nationality was invented, but it was after the military defeat in 1967 that it became a powerful weapon against Israel. This is because Israel had gained control of Gaza and the West Bank. Keep in mind, what had happened is that the Israelis had defeated the Muslims in a defensive war. In that war, they won a tiny portion of the vast territory which is controlled by the many Muslim nations.

The Muslims realized that by creating a new nationality in this small territory, they would make themselves the victims. Israel could not annex this land. The Israelis would not be taking a tiny piece of the massive Muslim land which they had won in a defensive war. Instead, the Israelis would be taking everything the Palestinians have left if they annex this land and do not give it back to the Palestinians.

The problem is that it is a lie, a deception. It is a different tactic following a military defeat, to destroy peaceful people who have tried to build a society with freedom and equality. Over time the world has come to accept that the Palestinians are a distinct and separate people. Judea and Samaria are now officially called the West Bank. The voices against Israel are far more numerous than the voices stating the truth.

Palestinians under the age of 60 have been called Palestinian all their life. They may genuinely see themselves as Palestinian, but the nationality was invented to vilify the Jews. It has been successful because of Jew-hatred in both the West and the Muslim world.

There are three types of Jew-hatred. One type comes from the political left, and it is the view that Jews are oppressors. Liberals view the world as a having a medieval-like class system where there are oppressors and the oppressed. According to the left, successful people are only successful because they oppress the poor.

Since the Israelis have built a prosperous society, the left views them as oppressors.

Historically, most humans have lived in a class system of some kind, but this is not universal. Today, in free societies some people may have more obstacles to overcome, but most successful people are successful through their own efforts.

This view of oppressor and oppressed comes from those with unearned wealth. It has a lot of adherents among the resentful poor, but it comes from those who inherited wealth and resent their parents. It comes from guilt and self-hatred by those unaware that most successful people earned their wealth.

This view of oppressor and oppressed causes the very evil it endlessly condemns. It is a collectivist view where people are judged based on the group they are identified with. Condemning people, not based on their sins, but based on the group identity you choose to assign them is evil. It does not matter if we group people by their skin color or if we group them based on their wealth or on the sins of their ancestors. Condemning people by their group identity is the cause of all slavery and genocide.

The second type of Jew-hatred comes from the political right, and it involves stupid conspiracy theories.

Jews are not successful because of a conspiracy but because God gave them some good advice. God gave the Jews the Torah and told them to study it. Everywhere they have gone, Jews are more likely than others to be literate. If you are going to study a book like your God requires, you must learn to read. The high literacy results in Jews learning many things, not just the Torah. This means that Jews have been among the most educated people everywhere they went.

God also gave the Jews the 10th commandment where they are told not to covet the property of others. This means they are not to be resentful of those who achieve success. It means that Jewish kids are brought up with the idea that being successful is not a bad thing. Being wealthy is not evil.

One problem with humans is that we always resent the success of others to some degree.

Poor kids are often taught that rich people are evil. They learn that if they become successful, they will be evil. Such kids are far less likely to be successful in life because they are far less likely to attempt to be successful.

Jews are more likely to be successful in life because they are more likely to try to be successful. They are often accused of being greedy because Jewish children are taught to believe that working hard and achieving wealth is not a sin. Jews are more likely to choose a career that can lead to greater prosperity. This is not evil "greed" or selfishness, it is merely being honest. It is an honest desire for a good life, as opposed to a resentment of those who have a good life. We should copy those who are successful, not resent them.

Success is not a sin, but being resentful of the success of others is a sin. This idea has greatly benefited the Jews. This is how the Jews were able to take wasteland and built an advanced civilization. The Jews did not oppress anyone as they built Israel by their intelligence and hard work.

The God of Israel also requires concern for the poor. When religion, the foundational worldview of a society encourages productivity and concern for the poor, the results can be better for the poor than any modern welfare state.

The God of Israel also requires compassion, ethics, morality, and justice. This is not to say that Jews are morally superior, but there is a difference between people and ideas. To understand some of the wisdom that is being revealed by God we must be able to discern the difference between people and ideas.

All people are equal in that all people should be treated equally. Human equality is an idea, but chattel slavery is a different and opposing idea. Chattel slavery is an idea that is evil, and inferior to the idea of human equality.

All people are equal, so it would have to be true that all ideas are not equal.

Some ideas are morally superior to other ideas. This does not mean that the people who hold inferior ideas are inferior people. We must distinguish between people and ideas. We should not allow the truth of human equality to cause us to be unable to see the difference between good ideas and bad ideas.

It can be difficult to distinguish between people and ideas because they are intertwined. The ideas that influence a community become part of the people in that community. Criticizing an ideology will somehow be seen by many as criticism of the people who believe in that ideology.

Muslims can be very hostile to criticism, sometimes violently hostile. Peaceful Muslims audaciously claim that they are the ones being attacked when someone merely criticizes their religion even while critics of Islam face actual violence. Some degree of hostility towards critics is reasonable, but the violent reaction by many Muslims to any criticism is one clear and undeniable example of evil in Islam. Extreme hostility to truthful criticism is evil, and it demonstrates that Islam is evil.

There are other examples of evil in Islam, but this does not mean Muslims are evil. It is the religion that is evil, not the people who follow it. People are influenced by their religion and all ideas they hold true, and sometimes people commit acts of violence because of their religious beliefs.

People will be held accountable, but the ideas that influence them are part of the spiritual warfare that is taking place in the world. People who commit evil because of an evil ideology can sometimes be good people who were born in the wrong society.

God did not choose Israel to be a superior people, but He gave them ideas that are superior. God gave the Jews a religion where there is a higher level of ethics, and greater success in life. It is greatly significate that Judaism is built on ideas which are good, while Islam is built on ideas which are evil. The conflict in the Middle East is not good people versus evil people, but a conflict between good ideas versus evil ideas.

Ideas are the battlefield of spiritual warfare. Spiritual forces may give ideas to humanity like the words given to the prophets in the Bible.

Spiritual forces may inspire ideas. Creation provides a manifestation of ideas and their effect. This is one purpose for creation, but it is more of a demonstration and not a learning experience for God. The Jews were chosen to be the guardians of good ideas. Good ideas lead to righteousness and joy, bad ideas lead to sin and suffering.

The third type of Jew-hatred comes from Islam. Islam is a religion that has some really bad ideas. This is not to criticize Muslims. As previously stated, we must be able to distinguish the difference between people and ideas even though most people cannot seem to do this. Muslims are people, but Islam is a religion. It is the ideas of Judaism that are good while the ideas of Islam are evil.

In Judaism the relationship between God and humans is paternal. God is our Father who loves us.

In Islam the relationship between God and humans is that of master and slaves. This gives a Divine sanction to chattel slavery by which devout followers of Islam will often believe in slavery. It was the West that forced the Muslim world to end slavery to the degree slavery was ended in the Muslim world. In Islam, chattel slavery is sanctioned by God, and Islamic groups like ISIS will restore slavery when they can.

Muslims may reject slavery by saying only God can hold slaves, but this is a weak argument. If God does not consider slavery to be wrong, then slavery is not wrong. Since the God of Islam has slaves, there will always be many Muslims who see slavery as perfectly honorable and righteous.

Death to apostates is another evil aspect of Islam. The percentage of Muslims who are engaged in violence is irrelevant. Mohammed gave very clear commands to kill apostates. There is a difference between people and ideas. Muslims are people who can be peaceful, Islam is a religion and violence is part of Islam. Christians can be violent, but violence is not a part of Christianity. When it comes to Islam, violence is part of the religion itself.

Another evil aspect of Islam is the deception. Mohammed said, "war is deceit.", and through repetition and greater numbers the enemies of Israel have used deception very effectively. Israel is falsely and endlessly accused of genocide and apartheid by people who do not care about the genocide and apartheid going on all around Israel.

People have come to believe that Israel is the aggressor even though conflict is always started by the Muslims. They are so greatly outnumbered it is unreasonable to claim that the Jews are the aggressor. It is astounding that so many people believe what is obviously a lie. As any reasonable person should expect, the greatly outnumbered Jews have gone to great effort to find peace with their enemies. Their enemies will not even concede the Jewish state's right to exist.

The lies against Israel are effective because of all the Jew-hatred. Conservative Jew-haters will look at Jewish success and say it is a conspiracy. Liberal Jew-haters will look at Jewish success and say the Jews are somehow oppressing the Palestinians. The real cause of Jew-hatred is resentment by which people believe the lies.

Islamic Jew-hatred seems supernatural. This confirms the spiritual warfare being played out in the conflict between Israel and Islam.

This condition in modern times, the tremendous hostility towards the Jews, and all the deception that is used against them, this would also be something for which Israel was chosen. Being "chosen" does not mean that the Jews are superior in the eyes of God but merely selected for the coming of Messiah. They were also chosen to hold a righteous religion given to them by God.

We should not hate the people on either side, we are all being influenced by spiritual forces. We should know that a story is being told here. Understanding is being revealed. In the beginning of the end, we see the Jews, chosen by God, hated by the world. They are almost surrounded, and greatly outnumbered by those who self-righteously believe that they serve god by using deception and whatever brutality is necessary to destroy a peaceful people. The Jews represent truth. They represent all good people. They hold the Torah, the word of God, and even though the world is against them, Israel, in the end, will be victorious.

The conflict in the Middle East is a conflict between truth and falsehood, the few against the many. It is a conflict between one religion which is small but believes in freedom, equality, knowledge, truth, compassion, and justice verses another religion which has a great multitude of followers but believes in inequality, subjugation, slavery, blind obedience, deception, and death. This is a conflict between life and death and some of the most devout Muslims will proudly state that they support death as much as the Jews support life.

This is history's clearest battle between good and evil. It is fundamentally not a battle of good people versus evil people. It is more of a conflict between good ideas versus evil ideas even though people are acting on those ideas, and people are responsible for their words and actions.

Because of deception, most humanity will support evil.

Amazing, but not surprising, most of the world is against Israel.

If you look at the whole story, starting with Abraham, it is a remarkable story. We do not know exactly how it's going to turn out, but everything points to the idea that God is not finished with Israel. Israel was selected for the coming of Christ, but Israel was also selected for what is happening now which very likely has to do with the return of Christ.

The Jews continue to wait for a Messiah who will arrive like a knight in shining armor, but the true story of the Messiah is more elaborate and more incredible than the simple outcome they are expecting.

Jesus will return to Jerusalem, and they will say blessed is He who comes in the name of the Lord.

Chapter 9 – The Truth is not Revealed until the End

It seems odd that Christ spoke so mysteriously. We should not have such unshakable confidence that what Christ decided not to tell us would be revealed by complicated theological theories developed centuries after His death.

Jesus said the Holy Spirit would be sent to guide us. Christians believe that the theology of the church they attend came from the Holy Spirit. The problem is that different theories have appeared and been refined over many centuries.

This being the case we cannot know when the correct information was revealed, or if it has been revealed. As different scholars have developed all the various interpretations of the Bible, we cannot know which of them, if any of them, were inspired by the Holy Spirit.

Christ decided to not clearly tell us how His suffering and death redeems us. Various theories of atonement have been developed, but the most widely believed theories today were developed many centuries after the death of Christ.

Overwhelmingly the early church tended to focus on the destruction of evil, or the destruction of death, or our being freed from the dominion of Satan as the means of our redemption. This is why the ransom theory became the most common view of atonement for one thousand years after Christ. Destroying death, or destroying evil, or freeing us from the dominion of Satan are merely slight variations of the same basic idea. This was a nearly universal view of atonement held by the early church.

Christ frees us from the dominion of Satan; this was how those who knew the apostles understood our atonement. The Catholic church abandoned this church tradition in the eleventh century as it moved away from the ransom theory. The ransom theory was the explanation for redemption, but the means of redemption was the destruction of evil. When the church abandoned the ransom theory explanation, it also abandoned the destruction of evil as the means of atonement.

This led to satisfaction atonement and eventually penal substitutionary atonement. Both are vicarious where the righteousness or suffering of Christ is applied to us. This ignores clear Biblical statements that God will not punish anyone for the sins of someone else. There were a few statements to suggest vicarious atonement in the early church, but such statements were not common. They were made by church fathers who espoused other means of atonement suggesting they were rhetorical and not literal.

The satisfaction theory of the Catholic church is less obviously vicarious than substitutionary atonement, but it is vicarious, and it originated many centuries after Christ. As a developed theory, penal substitutionary atonement dates to the Protestant Reformation which was just a few centuries ago.

If the Holy Spirit waited for centuries to reveal information, then information revealed in the twenty-first century would be as credible as information revealed in the eleventh century or the sixteenth century. Information revealed in the end would be more credible since there could be a reason for the timing.

The idea that Christ witnessed the hatred of Satan as explained in chapter one, provides a much better explanation for how Christ frees us from the dominion of Satan. This view of atonement is a return to the earliest church authority or the original church tradition. It explains the means of atonement that was taught by the early church.

God looked away from the crucifixion and Satan believed he could openly curse God without a witness. Jesus transcends Heaven and He is a witness against the devil. This may sound too simple, but we should expect the truth to be simple.

Theologians are very intelligent people who have developed several competing interpretations of the Bible. Their doctrines tend to be complex as they try to fit all the conflicting passages together.

Smart people overlook the simple things.

The Messiah was born to a poor teenager in a barn. God is the small still voice that spoke to Elijah. From many stories in the Bible, God seems to prefer the simple.

The Bible is not some super complex riddle that only a genius can solve. The solutions to some of the greatest mysteries in the Bible are amazingly simple. Some solutions are so simple that it is perhaps God's greatest miracle that He has prevented everyone from seeing them.

There may have been millions of times when a Christian considered the possibility that God the Father is outside of time, while God the Son moves in time. Such an idea would lead to the revelation that Jesus transcends Heaven, so God would simply cause such thoughts to be forgotten. The explanation for the Trinity will be revealed when God allows it to be revealed.

In Exodus, God spoke to the nation of Israel. A greater miracle is the silence over the last two thousand years. God has prevented Heaven and Earth from solving some simple riddles.

Isaiah 25:7 And he will destroy in this mountain the face of the covering cast over all people, and the vail that is spread over all nations.

God "vails" our eyes until the time of the end. This suggests that the solutions to the riddles of the Bible are not complicated. There are simple solutions that we should have been able to see. We could not see them because God did not want us to see them.

Isaiah 40:4-5 Every valley shall be exalted, and every mountain and hill shall be made low: and the crooked shall be made straight, and the rough places plain: And the glory of the Lord shall be revealed, and all flesh shall see it together: for the mouth of the Lord hath spoken it.

Mountains and hills will block a person's view. If the mountains are made low and the valleys are exalted, then the people will be able to see what they had not been able to see. They would have seen it, but their view was blocked.

This confirms that the truth is simple.

Mount Zion will not necessarily be on a mountain. Mount Zion could be referring to those who are able to see like those on a mountain. The lifting of a veil, and flattening the hills, both suggest a revelation of truth at the time of the end.

But why does God veil our eyes, and why is the truth revealed in the end times? Since the Bible is a book of riddles, there must be a reason for all the riddles. The solution must also explain why the truth was hidden in a riddle.

If we are to experience the full measure of sorrow in this life, we would have to be uncertain about the existence of God, and the afterlife. This would be necessary if the whole point of creation was for us, and for God, to experience emotions like sorrow.

Jesus had to die to return to the Father, and God had to forsake Him and look away. When Jesus was on the cross, forsaken by God, the devil openly cursed God. The devil believed he was safe with the face of God turned away. The devil is still in Heaven, still believing he is safe.

As it is revealed that Jesus is the Lord, at the Right Hand of God, transcending Heaven, Satan will at some point confront the Archangel Michael. Jesus is a witness against Satan. The devil will also realize that God is a witness against him. Christ returns to oneness with God. Since God transcends time, He is already a witness against the devil.

Luke 17:29-30 But the same day that Lot went out of Sodom it rained fire and brimstone from heaven, and destroyed them all. Even thus shall it be in the day when the Son of man is revealed.

It is the revelation of Jesus as Lord in Heaven that causes the end times. It causes the devil to be cast out into the Earth. This is why God veiled our eyes. This is why the Bible is given as a riddle. This secret had to be kept to the end because this revelation causes the end.

Several different atonement theories have been developed over the centuries. None of them can explain why Christ could not tell us how He redeems us. If Jesus died to ransom us, or if He died as a substitute, He could have clearly told us. Christ as a witness against the devil provides a reason for the secrecy.

The lifting of a veil, and the exalting of the valley are not the only clues that the Holy Spirit will reveal information in the end times.

One common theme in both the Old and New Testament is that the followers of God in the end times will sing a new song. A song tells a story, or it conveys a message. Being a new song means that it is a new message, a new revelation from God.

Psalms 98:1-3 O sing unto the LORD a new song; for he hath done marvellous things: his right hand, and his holy arm, hath gotten him the victory. The LORD hath made known his salvation: his righteousness hath he openly shewed in the sight of the heathen. He hath remembered his mercy and his truth toward the house of Israel: all the ends of the earth have seen the salvation of our God.

God remembers Israel, God reveals His salvation, and all the Earth sees the salvation of God. This is not talking about the New Testament, or anything revealed in the first century.

Christians tend to believe this "revelation of knowledge" often described in the Bible was fulfilled at the time of Christ. Certainly, there was knowledge revealed at that time, but Christ spoke in parables and clearly did not come for the purpose of revealing all knowledge, at least not during His first coming.

If Christianity can be said to have been taken to all the ends of the Earth, this certainly did not occur until many centuries after Israel was destroyed. Only in modern times when Israel has been restored can this passage be fulfilled literally.

It may be that God remembers Israel by the restoration of Israel. Perhaps God remembers Israel by some event yet to come but this could not occur until modern times. It could not have been fulfilled literally when Israel did not exist. Literal fulfillment is always more impressive. A literal fulfillment means this "new song" would have to come in modern times. It is unavoidable that any new revelation will conflict with some of the answers that religious scholars have developed over the centuries.

This new song or new message reveals how the right hand of God has gotten the victory. Christ is the Right Hand of God, the one who sits at the Right Hand of God. Christ has gotten the victory but according to this passage how He does it is not revealed or made known until the time of the end. This salvation, which is to say how Christ redeems us, will be seen by all the ends of the Earth.

An examination of the scriptures that relate to this "New Song" or this revelation of knowledge indicates that knowledge is to be revealed in the end times.

1 Peter 1:5 Who are kept by the power of God through faith unto salvation ready to be revealed in the last time.

This new message makes His salvation known. It reveals how the right hand of God has gotten the victory. References to the "new song" found in the book of Revelation confirms that this new song is revealed in the end times.

Revelation 5:8-10 And when he had taken the book, the four beasts and four and twenty elders fell down before the Lamb, having every one of them harps, and golden vials full of odours, which are the prayers of saints. And they sung a new song, saying, Thou art worthy to take the book, and to open the seals thereof: for thou wast slain, and hast redeemed us to God by thy blood out of every kindred, and tongue, and people, and nation; And hast made us unto our God kings and priests: and we shall reign on the earth.

One central theme of the new song is Christ and how He redeems His children. With this new message we learn that the redemption provided by Christ is not only for the Christian nations. It is for the children of God from all nations, peoples, and tongues.

Revelation 14:1-3 And I looked, and, lo, a Lamb stood on the mount Sion, and with him an hundred forty and four thousand, having his Father's name written in their foreheads. And I heard a voice from heaven, as the voice of many waters, and as the voice of a great thunder: and I heard the voice of harpers harping with their harps: And they sung as it were a new song before the throne, and before the four beasts, and the elders: and no man could learn that song but the hundred and forty and four thousand, which were redeemed from the earth.

Psalms 96:10-13 Say among the heathen that the LORD reigneth: the world also shall be established that it shall not be moved: he shall judge the people righteously. Let the heavens rejoice, and let the earth be glad; let the sea roar, and the fulness thereof. Let the field be joyful, and all that is therein: then shall all the trees of the wood rejoice Before the LORD: for he cometh, for he cometh to judge the earth: he shall judge the world with righteousness, and the people with his truth.

The new song is about how we are redeemed by Christ, yet the Lord shall judge the world with righteousness. It seems odd that there is a great celebration considering it says we will be judged righteously. Our being judged righteously should be a problem for us since we are part evil.

The Lord judges us with righteousness and this could only be good news if we are righteous. This means we are not only forgiven, but we are also righteous. Our flesh is discarded, and we are transformed into angels of God. We are sinless going forward, and worthy of eternal life in the perfect kingdom of God.

Another central theme of this new message is praise to the glory of God. The new song or new message reveals how God has done marvelous things. It reveals how the will of God is achieved in absolute completeness. God gives us our own free will. He judges everyone by their works. He destroys all evil and yet God redeems all His children.

God in His mercy redeems every tiny piece of love, and God in His justice destroys every tiny piece of evil. God wins in all things, and He loses none of His children. The purpose of creation is achieved, and God sets all things right. His will is achieved in all things.

The new song is the wonderful news that God is absolute Love, Mercy, and Justice beyond comprehension. There is no greater comfort than to know that God is in complete control. In all things, His will be done. This is what the first commandment is all about.

Psalm 85:11 Truth shall spring out of the earth; and righteousness shall look down from heaven.